Zabars

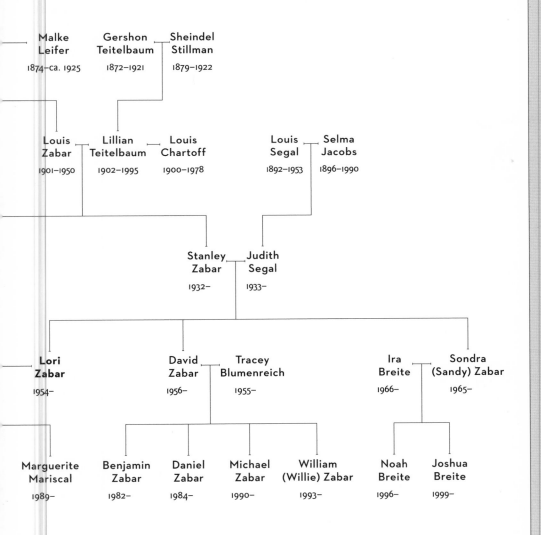

Malke Leifer
1874–ca. 1925

Gershon Teitelbaum
1872–1921

Sheindel Stillman
1879–1922

Louis Zabar
1901–1950

Lillian Teitelbaum
1902–1995

Louis Chartoff
1900–1978

Louis Segal
1892–1953

Selma Jacobs
1896–1990

Stanley Zabar
1932–

Judith Segal
1933–

Lori **Zabar**
1954–

David Zabar
1956–

Tracey Blumenreich
1955–

Ira Breite
1966–

Sondra (Sandy) Zabar
1965–

Marguerite Mariscal
1989–

Benjamin Zabar
1982–

Daniel Zabar
1984–

Michael Zabar
1990–

William (Willie) Zabar
1993–

Noah Breite
1996–

Joshua Breite
1999–

ZABAR'S

ZABAR'S

A FAMILY STORY, WITH RECIPES

LORI ZABAR

FOREWORD BY JULIA MOSKIN

SCHOCKEN BOOKS, NEW YORK

Grateful acknowledgment is made to Ethel Sheffer for permission
to reprint excerpts from "The Zabar Mystique" by Isaiah Sheffer.

The map on page xiii was drawn by Suleyman Sarihan at the Slavic
and Eastern Library, University of Illinois at Urbana-Champaign,
with the assistance of Merrily Shaw at the Russian, East European,
and Eurasian Center, University of Illinois at Urbana-Champaign.

Library of Congress Cataloging-in-Publication Data
Name: Zabar, Lori, author.
Title: Zabar's : a family story, with recipes / Lori Zabar;
foreword by Julia Moskin.
Description: New York, NY : Schocken Books, 2022. Includes index.
Identifiers: LCCN 2021045945 (print) | LCCN 2021045946 (ebook) |
ISBN 9780805243390 (hardcover) | ISBN 9780805243406 (ebook)
Subjects: LCSH: Gourmet food industry—New York (State)—New York.
Zabar's & Co.—History. Families—Biography.
Classification: LCC HD9005 .Z33 2022 (print) | LCC HD9005 (ebook) |
DDC 338.4/764795097471—dc23/eng/20211109
LC record available at https://lccn.loc.gov/2021045945
LC ebook record available at https://lccn.loc.gov/2021045946

www.schocken.com

Printed in the United States of America
First Edition
1st Printing

TO MY PARENTS, JUDY AND STANLEY ZABAR—

You told me the world was my oyster and I could do anything.

This book—the pearl—is for you.

CONTENTS

At a conservative estimate, I am 75 to 80 percent Zabar's.

I was a baby when my family moved to the Upper West Side in 1968, and Zabar's was the first food destination of what became many. As I grew up to be a food writer and then a reporter for the Food section of *The New York Times*, I was lucky enough to have astonishing tastes of food that ranged from freshly pulled buffalo milk mozzarella in Italy to wild tomatoes in the Yucatàn to spherified olives in Spain.

But all of that laid end to end wouldn't begin to match my lifetime consumption of just Zabar's cream cheese, whitefish salad, and smoked salmon (hand-sliced, of course). Not to mention the bagels, the rugelach, and the bites of real English Cheddar, Greek olives, and Turkish pistachio nuts along the way.

The iconic Zabar's orange-and-brown shopping bag was my earliest reading material; among my first words were "Gaspé salmon" and "herring in cream sauce," a dish I dreaded and feared as a child because of its murky appearance. In the 1960s, my parents dived deep into the food revolution: they named me after Julia Child, joined one of the city's first farm co-ops, and schlepped us to Astoria for whole grilled fish, to Flushing for incendiary Sichuan stews, and beyond. Zabar's always welcomed me home with its familiar coffee-scented air, sawdust-covered floors, and salami and garlic braids hanging overhead.

Like most traditional appetizing stores, Zabar's specialized in preserved, pickled, and dried food, from salted fish to cured cheeses to dried fruit. As a somewhat confused second-generation American Jew, I was always mystified by the fact that Zabar's also stocked Italian prosciutto and Virginia ham, and made a magnificent dish of poached shrimp in dill sauce. But it was the late twentieth century, and all kinds of cultural and culinary assimilation were happening. The local Chinese restaurants were packed with Jews trying shrimp with lobster sauce, pork fried rice, and other nonkosher dishes they would never cook at home. Jewish deli owners started offering cheese in their meat sandwiches (at Katz's Deli downtown, the family debated for years before putting a Reuben on the menu) and "kosher-style," like the food at Zabar's, was born.

All the regular shoppers knew that Louis and Lillian Zabar, Jewish immigrants from Eastern Europe, had opened the store in 1934. We could tell Saul and Stanley, the scions who have worked there since boyhood, apart by sight. In the 1970s, we were shaken by the Great Schism that propelled the youngest brother, Eli, to leave and bake his own breads—on the Upper East Side, our sworn cultural rival.

But no one, including the Zabars themselves, knew exactly how the geopolitical upheavals of twentieth-century Europe had transported Mordko Leib Zabarka and Leika Teitelbaum from a precarious life in preindustrial Ukraine to a prosperous one as Louis and Lillian Zabar, living in a classic six on the Upper West Side. Although its outlines are familiar to many Ashkenazi Jews like me, who were saved from poverty, pogroms, and the Holocaust by the courage of our immigrant ancestors, the story is still astounding to read.

Before she became the family's unofficial historian, Lori Zabar was famous in her household for mastering the art of filleting a whole smoked whitefish at age four. She brought the same thoroughness to this project, finding databases and documents that the family had been unaware of. I was riveted by her account of the Zabarka family's life in the shtetl of Ostropolia, especially its heartbreaking and violent end at the hands of Cossack soldiers and local anti-Semites. And I was deeply envious to learn what it's like to grow up as a Zabar: being given the run of the store and allowed to eat anything you see (except for the caviar and smoked sturgeon—too expensive even for the royal offspring).

I now see that I've led a sheltered life, rarely living more than a mile from Zabar's. On my first trip away from home, I flew to Vancouver bearing the only house gift I knew of: a full spread of Zabar's bagels, smoked fish, and cream cheese. (All three flavors! Plain, scallion, and vegetable!) It did not occur to me, despite the fact that the family I was visiting had lived only in India and Saudi Arabia before settling in Canada, that they might not fall upon this with joy. My new friend's mother, a magnificent cook, eyed the spread politely. "Let me understand," she said, "you eat the fish and the cheese together on the bread, all at the same time?" My cheeks flamed, my toes curled; I had never seen my foundational foods as strange before.

I've thought about that moment many times in the course of my work, using it to remind myself that foods that seem alien at first— sea urchin, horse meat, fish balls—are not so different from the gefilte fish, smoked sturgeon, and chicken livers that I was raised on. And that the Eastern European flavors of the Zabar's kitchen— foods such as horseradish, mustard, and caraway seeds—are close relatives of chiles, wasabi, and cumin.

When I moved back to the neighborhood as an adult, Zabar's had evolved: it was now a repository of global flavors, a tourist destination, and also a useful place for a parent to buy bribes for a child, such as Russian coffee cake and Chinese roast pork buns. The Zabar family's commitment to traditional, handmade foods has stood firm, making it possible for me to introduce my children to such beloved touchstones as air-dried salami, half-sour pickles, and raw-milk cheese. (They have never developed a taste for herring in cream sauce, though.)

But I'm most grateful to Zabar's simply for being there, for keeping the culinary connection to my heritage alive. The other food emporiums that helped shape New York's culinary revolution in the 1970s and 1980s—Balducci's, Dean & DeLuca, DDL Foodshow, Macy's Cellar—are gone. The businesses that fed the Upper West Side of my childhood—Bartons candy store, Steinberg's dairy restaurant, Schrafft's soda fountain, Oppenheimer's butcher shop— are gone. But Zabar's, largely because it's still owned and run by its founding family, has survived. Saul is still in charge of the coffee and smoked fish, Stanley continues to oversee the business side, Stanley's son David fills the executive director post, Saul's son Aaron carries on as a manager, and Lillian and Louis's great-grandson Willie manages the social media accounts, keeping Zabar's in the public eye.

The Internet went crazy when longtime Upper West Side congressman Jerry Nadler was spotted carrying a Zabar's shopping bag onto the floor of the House of Representatives on January 13, 2021, the day of Donald Trump's second impeachment. Asked the next day by a reporter what the bag contained, a Nadler staffer replied, "A babka and a copy of the U.S. Constitution, what else?"

During the winter of 2020, at one of the heights of the COVID-19 pandemic, spotting Saul in the store collecting shopping carts and seeing Stanley walking the sales floor on the eve of Hanukkah was a light in the darkness, a literal sign of survival. The threads connecting American Jews to our old-country ancestors grow ever thinner, but in my family, like in many, food is one of the strongest. Bagels, cream cheese, and lox still nourish our funerals and birthdays, our graduations and reunions, our circumcisions and care packages. To us, Zabar's is the taste of life itself.

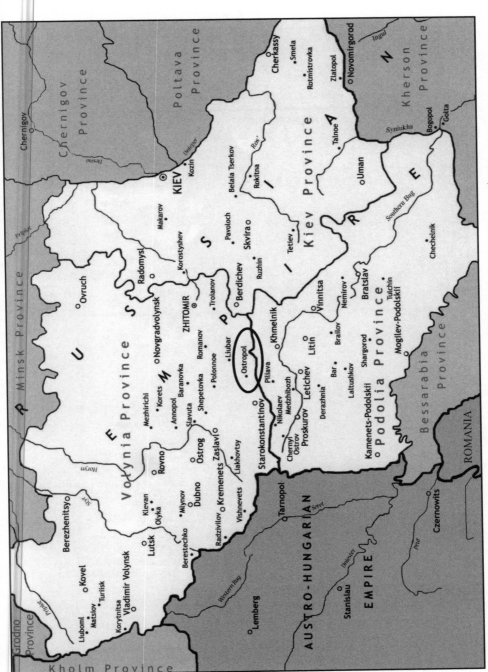

The Volynia, Podolia, and Kiev provinces of the Russian Empire, around 1900.

INTRODUCTION

"Can I ask you a question?"

I've become accustomed to hearing this from people who have just been introduced to me. I usually beat them to the punch by replying, "Yes, I'm related to the store." And to their inevitable follow-up query, I answer, "It was started by my grandparents in 1934."

No matter how often I experience this exchange, the interest in my family's business is always gratifying. These people know Zabar's as one of the world's greatest gourmet food stores, celebrated in books, in films, and on television, but they are amazed to learn that it has been at its original Broadway location for more than eighty-five years and that it is still being run by the same family who founded it—something that is quite unusual in today's big-business environment.

My paternal grandparents, Lillian Teitelbaum and Louis (pronounced Louie) Zabar, fled the pogroms and unrest in Russia before they were a couple and arrived in the United States in 1921 and 1922, respectively. With little but willpower and a keen business sense, they built a retail food business that eventually consisted of Zabar's and four grocery stores, all located along Broadway on the Upper West Side of Manhattan, from 80th Street to 110th Street. When my grandfather died in 1950 at the age of forty-nine, the businesses were taken over by his older sons—my uncle Saul and my father, Stanley—along with their eventual partner, Murray Klein. Together, the trio developed the company's offerings and its real estate until Zabar's was not only an iconic food store on the Upper West Side but also one of the most famous delicatessens in the world. Zabar's is a cultural landmark and a vestige of Old New York that has survived nearly a century of transformation. You can't miss that four-story, white-stucco, and brown-wood gabled Tudor-style structure that takes up half a city block, and the store's classic bright orange banner.

Every day, thousands of loyal local customers and tourists from across America and all over the world stream into the store for their weekly roast of fresh coffee; for a yeasty chocolate babka or tender, raisin-filled rugelach; for flaky potato knishes or blintzes plump with fruit; for cheeses of all kinds; and, on weekends, for Zabar's legendary New York bagels with nova and a schmear. Some keep coming back because they love the store's chaotic energy or because the food reminds them of their childhood fare. Others have purposely moved to the neighborhood because of its "PTZ" (proximity to Zabar's).

Like many of these customers, I'm also an Upper West Sider who pushes her cart through the store's narrow, jam-packed aisles several times a week. Customers have their own rituals for shopping at Zabar's, and here is mine.

My first stop is often just inside the store, at the bins of glistening olives—ebony, brown, and green—from France, Italy, Greece, Tunisia, Morocco, and beyond. I fill a container with my selections: intensely salty, wrinkled ebony Nyons; meaty, mild Cerignolas as large as golf balls; and my personal favorite, the petite and piquant French pitted Niçoise. Most people nibble them with a glass of wine before dinner, but I like to toss them into a mixed salad.

Next, I head to the staggering cheese selection. On my right, behind a serviced counter that extends nearly three yards, is a wall of hard cheeses—wheels of nutty Irish Cheddar, buttery Spanish Manchego, and sweeter Grana Padano. In the display case in front of the counter are the softer cheeses, dozens of them, mostly French and some Spanish, English, and American, cut into wedges large and small. Opposite the counter, on long steel racks, is a multitude of packaged and precut cheeses of various nationalities.

If I need guidance, I seek out Olga Dominguez, the department manager, who comes from the Dominican Republic and has been at the store since 1972. Olga's best guess is that there are more than one thousand cheeses for sale at Zabar's, the most popular being goat cheeses and alpine cheeses such as Swiss and Gruyère. Among my favorites are Oma, a pungent and sweet washed-rind cheese made from organic milk produced by the von Trapp family cows in Vermont (yes, that's the *Sound of Music* von Trapp family; after they left Europe for America in 1939, they eventually established a farm and resort in Stowe, Vermont); Humboldt Fog, a mold-ripened goat's milk cheese with a central line of edible white ash from California; and Reblochon, a soft, raw cow's milk cheese originating in the alpine region of Savoy in France.

Incredible cheese requires artisanal bread. The Zabar's bread and bakery department offers everything from superb baguettes and all varieties of bagels to loaves of country sourdough, semolina, whole wheat, and raisin walnut bread, not to mention rolls, muffins, croissants, babkas, and cookies. Zabar's own rye bread is so delicious that my Upper East Side friends take the crosstown bus to buy it. I, on the other hand, can't come here without purchasing a half pound of cinnamon rugelach, a golden-brown crescent-shaped pastry made from cinnamon, nuts, and raisins that have been rolled into a cream cheese dough.

The bounteous prepared-food section is at the back of the store. Here, too, the choices are a gastronomic United Nations of more than twenty rotating selections, including beef bourguignon, shepherd's pie, lasagna, potato latkes, Texas-style ribs, rotisserie chicken and duck, and poached salmon with dill sauce, as well as traditional deli meats and chicken soup with matzoh balls. It's all prepared by three dozen cooks and assistants who toil from morning to night in two sizable kitchens in the back of the store. The menus change frequently, according to the seasons, holidays, and special events. Things begin to get particularly boisterous in this part of the store at about 6:00 p.m., when crowds of hungry customers clutching numbered tickets wait for their turn to point, grab, and go home with their dinner.

Past the prepared foods is a Zabar's staple—the coffee station. Zabar's is renowned for coffee that is both high quality and moderately priced, which may be why they sell between eight and ten thousand pounds a week, in the store and online. The coffee department boasts twenty-eight wooden barrels filled to the brim with shiny beans in shades of russet, tan, black, and brown that have been sourced from countries all over the world. My personal favorite is a subtly flavored hazelnut, but most customers love the basic Zabar's roast, which is smooth and intense but not the least bit bitter. The coffee beans are blended and roasted to the store's exacting requirements—which is to say, to the specifications of my uncle Saul, the family's coffee aficionado. Saul was one of the initiators, if not the initiator, of the 1960s gourmet coffee movement.

All of this is just a warm-up before I proceed to the very heart of the store: the appetizing department, which includes Zabar's legendary smoked fish. Smoked fish is so important in the lives of many of our customers that it has on occasion inspired declarations of romantic love right in front of the counter. Zabar's most popular commodity has always been salmon, in all of its luscious varieties: cured, smoked, baked, poached, and kippered, or prepared as lox, Nova Scotia, Scotch smoked, or gravlax. Alongside the salmon, with their own fanatically devoted fan base, are Zabar's herring, sable, and sturgeon, and, last but not least, sturgeon caviar. To this day, Saul and Tomas Rodriguez, manager of the department and assistant buyer, personally select all the fish that Zabar's sells, and they frequently reject whatever is not up to their strict standards. I order a half pound of Nova Scotia from counterman James Bynum, who offers me a taste as he slices and as we update each other about our children and banter about current events. Just as some people have favorite bartenders or favorite barbers, some of Zabar's customers have their special counterman, and they will wait patiently, for however long it takes, until he is available. James's station is at the right end of the long fish counter; this spot and the one on the opposite end are reserved for the store's most gifted slicers. Slicing fish is serious business, and it takes many months, even years, to reach a level of skill worthy of Zabar's. An expert slicer produces gossamer slices thin enough, it is said, to read *The New York Times* through. James's hand-sliced Nova Scotia, rather than the prepackaged variety, is worth the wait. When I get back home, I will eat mine unconventionally, on a toasted sesame bagel with a layer of Zabar's whitefish salad and a slice of tomato.

After finishing at the appetizing counter, I go upstairs to The Mezzanine because I need to replace the glass pot in my Capresso drip coffee maker. The Zabar's housewares showroom is among the best stocked and least expensive in New York. It's the kind of place you visit in search of a rolling pin and leave with a milk foamer, a sauté pan, a paring knife, and an avocado slicer. Quiet, enthusiastic Bernardo Muniz—the current housewares manager, born in Puerto Rico and a Zabar's employee for thirty-seven years—is a walking kitchenwares catalog who can guide you through eighteen types of blenders and fifty different models of coffee makers, from a twenty-five-dollar plastic French press to a two-thousand-dollar behemoth that does everything but harvest the beans.

On my way out, I often drop by the Zabar's Cafe next door, which opened in 1979. Actually, it's more like a tiny self-service diner: long and narrow, with a communal counter, tall stools running the length of the room, and a central high-top rectangular table surrounded by more stools. When the cafe is busy, which is always, customers nudge their way around seated patrons and past a refrigerated case filled with bagels and nova, whitefish salad, and fresh-squeezed orange juice to the glass counter along the long northern wall. There they can order freshly brewed coffee, many of the baked goods found in the store, as well as warm egg sandwiches, panini, and frozen yogurt. Snagging a stool isn't as difficult as it seems, as customers come and go quickly. If you get a perch, chances are you will be privy to two or three opinionated conversations, often among total strangers. Some regulars meet there every day to schmooze over coffee and a croissant, which means I frequently run into my relatives, neighborhood friends, or acquaintances I've known for years. I've often thought that it makes the Upper West Side seem like my grandparents' shtetl.

To the devoted customers I encounter on these visits, Zabar's is almost as deeply embedded in their family histories as it is in mine. Nora Ephron, who considered Zabar's the "ultimate West Side institution," once confessed in *The New York Times* that her fantasy was to actually *be* a Zabar. My mother read this and promptly invited her to brunch.

I can't invite all of our devotees to brunch, but I can share our

Zabar's legendary cheese counter.

story. It's not just a family story, a business story, a Jewish story, or even a New York story, but a uniquely American story. It encompasses one hundred years of family folklore, behind-the-scenes anecdotes of beloved employees and quirky customers, original Zabar-family recipes (some of which became mainstays of the store), and the evolution of the Upper West Side from bustling upper-middle-class Jewish neighborhood to down-at-the-heels and sometimes dangerous area to today's thriving community of professionals and their families. A century after my grandparents immigrated to America, their great-grandchildren work in the business they founded and their legacy remains very much alive. This remarkable heritage includes four generations and counting of resilience, creativity, hard work, and strong family bonds. And let's not leave out religious persecution, municipal fines, some time spent in jail, at least one blackmailer, and plenty of smoked fish.

ZABAR'S

Ostropolia

I AM THE OLDEST OF LILLIAN AND LOUIS ZABAR'S EIGHT GRANDCHIL-dren. In the Ashkenazic European Jewish tradition, a child is often given the name of a deceased relative, but never a living one. Because many of those Yiddish-based European names sounded quaint and old-fashioned to first-generation Americans, it became the custom to come up with a name for a newborn that used just the first letter of the departed's name, so I was named Lori after my grandfather Louis, who died four years before I was born in 1954. Although I was close to my grandmother Lilly, who died in 1995 at age ninety-three, I grew up knowing little about my grandparents' childhoods in Russia or their early years in America. To understand how these two immigrants from a small Russian shtetl created an institution synonymous with cosmopolitan Jewish New York, I relied on my skills as an art historian and retired attorney. I interviewed relatives and Zabar's employees, did research in libraries, including the Center for Jewish History and the New York Public Library, and mined digital genealogical, municipal, and newspaper archives.

What I know about my grandfather's formative years came from stories that had been passed down by my grandmother; by Louis's sisters, my great-aunts Ada and Rose; by my parents and my uncles Saul and Eli; and what I'd heard from my cousins. They all agreed that my grandfather was a complex man: gruff, kind, generous, demanding, temperamental, charismatic, loyal, ambitious, and stubborn.

Louis Zabar was born Mordko (which is the Russian equivalent of the Hebrew Mordechai) Leib Zabarka in 1901 in Ostropolia (the

Yiddish version of Ostropol), which at the time was part of Czarist Russia and is now located in Ukraine. One of many small towns nestled in the province of Volynia, in 1901 Ostropolia was home to 10,000 inhabitants, 2,800 of whom were Jews. Encircled by crystalline lakes, dense pine forests, fragrant orchards, and rich farmland, it is bisected by a narrow, winding river called the Sluch. The closest major city, Kiev, is some 140 miles southwest, and at the time, the nearest railroad was 30 miles away in Polonnoe. Virtually all of Ostropolia's three hundred Jewish families lived in the town's historic center. Despite their geographic isolation and the restrictions the government had placed on travel and professions for Jews, Ostropolia's Jews were active participants in the local economy. They maintained ninety shops, where they traded with one another and with the gentiles who lived in town or on farms in the surrounding countryside, and they worked for and traded with a small group of wealthy gentiles who owned estates. They also were employed by the flour and corn mills, the main businesses of the region.

Louis's father, Schlomo Zabarka, was a big *macher,* a man of consequence. Born in 1870, Schlomo was an entrepreneur, both a retailer and a trader, who maintained a lumberyard on the grounds of the family home. His partner managed the lumber enterprise while Schlomo traveled throughout Ukraine with a hired driver and horse-drawn carriage, buying and selling commodities such as wheat, nuts, and butter, and supplies that included construction materials and apothecary jars.

Ukraine was at that time part of an area that had been designated by the Russian government in the eighteenth century as the Pale of Settlement (territory that fell within what had been Ukraine, Poland, Lithuania, Belarus, and Moldova, as well as western Russia), in which the Jews of the Russian Empire were forced to live. The 4.2 million Jews residing there were not allowed to travel beyond the Pale, and if they were caught doing so, they were arrested and returned in chains. Despite the risk, Schlomo broke this rule when he felt he needed to, journeying to Austrian-controlled Galicia, for example, to secure butter during a shortage. Schlomo was a yeller, a man who screamed until things were done to his satisfaction, and he brusquely mentored young Louis (whom he called Leib) in the ways of the commercial world. Louis, a strong, stocky boy, with dark wavy hair and piercing blue eyes, was an enthusiastic pupil.

While Schlomo traversed the Pale five days a week, his wife, Malke, was at home with Louis and his siblings. Malke was not Schlomo's first wife. At eighteen, Schlomo had married a sixteen-year-old named Bayla, who in short order presented him with a son whom they named Duvid, or "Dudie." In 1890, when Dudie was two, Bayla passed away from unknown causes. Five years later, Schlomo married twenty-one-year-old Malke Leifer. They had eight children: Gittel, Ada, Louis, Rose, Chana, Elka, Pessya, and Opryk (this seems to have been a Russian version of Aaron), who was nicknamed Archik.

Because no one in my family had ever discussed it in detail, I assumed my grandfather's childhood resembled the poor, deeply observant shtetl existence depicted in *Fiddler on the Roof,* but in fact his early life was comfortable and relatively modern. I began to revise my perception of the Zabarkas' lifestyle when I first saw a tinted photograph of Malke and Schlomo. They were dressed not in traditional ultra-Orthodox Jewish garb but in contemporary clothes. Malke is not wearing a wig, which many married Ortho-

Schlomo and Malke Zabarka in Ostropolia,
circa 1915–20. (ZABAR FAMILY COLLECTION)

dox women use to cover their hair; her straight hair is combed back from a pretty, fine-featured face with a smooth complexion. Schlomo's salt-and-pepper mustache and beard are neatly trimmed, he does not wear the traditional peyos, or sidelocks, and he is not wearing a yarmulke. The Zabarka family was knowledgeable about Judaism and observant, but not rigidly so.

Schlomo and Malke's clan shared a large, two-family house with his older brother and sister-in-law, Avrum and Fayga Kaliner Zabarka, and their five children, who from their pictures appeared to be more traditionally observant than Schlomo and Malke. Most of the residences in the center of Ostropolia were one-story wood buildings with dirt floors and straw-thatched roofs; a large central room served as a dining room, bedroom, and workroom. Wealthier families like the Zabarkas occupied larger houses, with more rooms, additional furniture, and maybe wood floors. But even in their large home the Zabarka children slept two to a bed, everyone trekked to an outhouse in the backyard, and bathing was done in a community bathhouse, no matter how frigid the temperature. As in all Russian households of that time, their kitchen featured a huge enclosed masonry fireplace that served as cookstove, oven, and heater. And when covered with feather beds, the expansive flat top of the fireplace provided a warm and cozy refuge on winter nights. The Zabarka domicile sat at the end of a block of houses, strategically located atop a sloping green field that bordered the Sluch River, where timber was floated to Schlomo's lumberyard. My great-aunt Ada remembered friends and family frolicking in the river in summer and skidding to school on its frozen surface in winter. Children were doted upon by the Jewish community, many of whose members were related by marriage. In the early decades of the twentieth century, Ostropolia was a happy place in which to grow up.

Despite the family's relative wealth, my great-grandmother worked hard at home, raising nine children with the help of a single maid. Every morning Malke milked the cow and then lugged the heavy pail to the kitchen for breakfast. As a reward for draining their glasses, Malke gave each child a kopek, except for Louis—he got two kopeks. My grandfather was Malke's favorite; until Archik was born in 1912, he was her only son. Ada joked that her mother gave Louis the extra kopek as a form of insurance for her soul; for traditional Jews, it is the sons who are obligated to say the Mourner's Kaddish every day for eleven months after a parent dies.

"Even back then," Ada added, "my brother was rich and I wasn't."

From what I've gathered from my family, Malke wasn't exactly a *balabusta* (a housewife who excels at cooking and household chores). Small and soft-spoken, the opposite of Schlomo in personality and manner, Malke had grown up in an intellectual family, and after her marriage still read avidly, including the few Jewish newspapers that managed to make their way to Ostropolia and were passed from family to family. She would gather the children and read them Bible stories and traditional tales of the Jewish holidays. While Schlomo was praying in shul on Saturday mornings, when no work was allowed, Malke's relatives and friends often dropped by to discuss Sholem Aleichem's latest story or Tolstoy's novels. Ada remembered her mother asking her opinion of Anna Karenina's choice to commit suicide. When she shared this in a recorded interview with her son Steve, I was struck by the fact that my great-grandmother and I had read and been deeply affected by the same book, six decades and an ocean apart. For the first time, I felt a kind of connection to her.

It was in the home of Malke's brother Lazar that Ostropolia's educated Jewish men gathered to talk, read newspapers, and ascertain what was happening in the greater Jewish world. The nascent Zionist movement, which had as its goal the establishment of a Jewish homeland in what was then known as Palestine, was gaining adherents among Europe's Jews at this time; they had been terrorized by pogroms and other manifestations of antisemitism for as long as anyone could remember. Unsurprisingly, there were Zionists among the Jews of Ostropolia; Gittel and Ada, the eldest Zabarka girls, even engaged a tutor to study modern Hebrew, as it was spoken in Palestine.

The Zabarkas and other progressive families in Ostropolia sent their children to the local Talmud Torah, a modern coed grammar school that taught both secular and Jewish subjects. Unlike the often grim and run-down traditional all-male religious schools, or *kheyders,* which were notorious for poor teaching and rote lessons, the Talmud Torah was housed in a large white building with spacious, clean classrooms and employed teachers who used modern educational methods. It was here that Louis Zabarka met petite, hazel-eyed Leika Teitelbaum, who would eventually become my grandmother Lilly. Lilly was a classmate of Louis's sister Rose and one year behind Louis in school; they got to know each other when Louis, who was always hungry, would sometimes share the apples he brought to school with his sister and her pretty friend.

Lilly's parents operated a tavern in Ostropolia that catered to a local clientele, including a good number of gentiles. (At the time, Jews were forbidden to own taverns within the Pale, but the authorities usually looked the other way.) Her father, Gershon, was a sweet and gentle man from an affluent family. Gershon had been blinded in a childhood accident, and so running the business fell to Lilly's capable mother, Sheindel. While her mother worked in the tavern, Lilly often kept her father company, going with him on walks and taking him to the synagogue. Lilly, who was several years younger than her brother Mottel, later described herself as the pampered baby of the household.

Slaking the peasants' thirst for alcohol was lucrative but hazardous. A roomful of volatile, inebriated men was not always the safest work environment. Brawls often broke out and, not infrequently, whichever Jews were in the vicinity became targets for the gentiles' indiscriminate rage. On those occasions, a frightened Lilly would race out the back of the tavern, to the house of her friend Rose Zabarka. Over time, Lilly got to know more of the Zabarka family. Rose, with her fair complexion, raven hair, and forceful, direct personality, resembled Schlomo and Louis. Pretty, pink-cheeked, and kindly Ada took after Malke.

Once they completed Talmud Torah, Russian high school followed for the Zabarka clan—free for gentiles, but not for the Jews. After high school, for those who could afford it, came the *gymnasye,* a more advanced level of education that prepared students for a university or professional school. Prior to the Russian Revolution in 1917, it was difficult for Jews to gain admission to *gymnasyes;* the government put a quota of 10 percent on Jews permitted in each class. When the czar was deposed by the Bolsheviks, Schlomo took advantage of the loosening of these restrictions and the ability of Jews to now travel beyond the Pale of Settlement to enroll his children and his nieces and nephews in *gymnasyes* and pay everyone's tuition. In Odessa, Louis studied at the S. N. Kononovich School, a private boys' *gymnasye,* Ada pursued a pharmacology degree and worked part-time in a pharmacy, and Rose, the bookish Zabarka, studied French and the classics. Lilly also proudly attended the *gymnasye* in Odessa. She may have followed a similar course of study, but I can't remember her ever uttering a word of *la belle langue*.

While the Zabarkas and Lilly were studying in Odessa, Russia remained in turmoil. World War I was over, but the Russian Revolution continued with the Red Army, the White Russians, Ukrainian nationalists, and assorted factions battling one another for power. The Russians and the Poles fought over large swathes of Ukraine, just as they had done for centuries. The Poles prevailed after two years of bloodshed, during which time hundreds of pogroms erupted against the Jews—for their supposed disloyalty to whomever was in charge at the moment, for their money or goods, or, most commonly, simply because they were Jews.

By 1919, Odessa was sinking into anarchy. Lilly had returned to her family by this time, and the chaos prompted Louis and Rose to do the same. The two Zabarkas matriculated at the *gymnasye* in Ostropolia, intending to stay close to home as things unspooled inside the Pale and beyond.

In addition to his studies, Louis continued to assist his father with his businesses. When Schlomo was away, Louis maintained the lumber business, delivered wood in a horse-drawn cart, and sold lumber and groceries at the house alongside his father's employees. In spite of the uncertainty and danger, eighteen-year-old Louis also traveled occasionally, even going as far as Romania to buy cherries.

But beginning in July 1919, local peasants, bandits, and followers of splinter political groups took advantage of the governmental turmoil to begin robbing, molesting, and killing the Jews of Ostropolia. The Jewish men, including my grandfather, organized a secret militia to patrol the community.

For a week in September 1920, beginning on the eve of Yom Kippur and extending through Sukkot, Louis nervously watched the retreating Bolshevik troops tramp through Ostropolia. Jews living in shtetls across Ukraine had encountered these armies before, crisscrossing their communities on their way to and from the front, plundering from the townspeople food, horses, and anything else they could use, leaving carnage and scarcity in their wake. Now, in Ostropolia, Cossacks allied with the Red Army arrested the town's Jewish leaders to extort money from them, even though many Jewish residents were already destitute. They looted stores and literally took the clothing off people's backs, leaving them naked and barefoot. The cries that arose from the streets terrified the Zabarkas and their neighbors as they huddled fearfully in their homes.

On a cold day at the end of Sukkot, the Zabarkas listened as the sound of clomping boots came nearer to their house. Then the front door was thrust open and a band of armed Cossack soldiers, accompanied by some local thugs, marched into the living room and demanded money. Schlomo complied as quickly as he could, hoping they would move on. But then several soldiers approached Malke and began groping her. When Schlomo tried to shield her with his body, one of the attackers became enraged and thrust his sword into Schlomo. As shots were fired and the blood began to flow, eight-year-old Archik slipped through a window to safety. Rose hid under a bed in a back room. Malke was frozen in shock, and two neighbors named Benjamin and Abe, who had been in the house along with the Zabarkas, tried to run away in the chaos. All three were shot. The two men died on the spot, but Malke, shot in the face, managed to stay conscious as blood poured out of her. Sixteen-year-old Chana, who had been outside when the shooting started, ran into the house and screamed when she saw her father slumped on the floor, the two dead men, and her bleeding mother. She was immediately shot dead as well.

Louis, who had been in the outhouse during the melee, heard the shrieks and ran into the house through the back door to retrieve the rifle he kept hidden under his bed. As the soldiers and bandits exited the front door, my grandfather chased after them, shooting as he ran. They shot back, but Louis was able to dodge the bullets and escaped into a nearby cellar, where he hid for several days.

Louis was told that Schlomo had bled to death hours after the attack and that Chana, Benjamin, and Abe had also been killed. He knew that his attempt to defend his family and his possession of a contraband weapon had made him a wanted man. He would have to flee Ostropolia.

Sympathetic peasants offered him passage out of town in a horse-drawn wagon. Jouncing along in the cart, concealed under a prickly pile of hay, my grandfather seethed and mourned. When a group of hostile peasants stopped the drivers, angrily poking their rifles and pitchforks into the hay, Louis held his breath, his heart racing. Luck saved him again: they missed.

Forced to lay low in another town, Louis wished he could come out of hiding to console his wounded mother and surviving siblings. He became even angrier when he learned that the soldiers and local bandits had been led to their door by a gentile acquaintance of the family who lived in a nearby village.

A week after the pogrom in the Zabarka household, a delegate arrived from the Joint Distribution Committee (JDC), an aid organization funded largely by American Jews. He had come to Ostropolia offering transport for young people who wanted to leave. Rose accepted the offer. She was soon on her way to Warsaw, preparing to immigrate to America.

BACK IN OSTROPOLIA, two days of quiet had followed the violence. Dazed survivors went through the heartbreaking rituals of burying family members and friends. They had barely concluded when the assailants returned to pick up where they'd left off. Once again, they entered homes, smashed furniture, and ripped open feather beds, rummaging for loot. Assisted by local peasants, the thieves filled their wagons with household goods and valuables and then departed.

On the following Monday, market day in Ostropolia, peasants calmly displayed their goods, as if nothing had happened. Nearby,

Jewish merchants did the same. Astoundingly, several bandits who were known to be among the killers roamed the market freely.

A delegation of Jews approached them, offering money in exchange for peace. One of the conciliators was Louis's uncle Lazar Leifer. The bandits took the money, but then ordered Lazar to lead them to his house. Fearing they would violate his grown daughter, he led them aimlessly through narrow side streets while pondering his next move. Angered by Lazar's meanderings, one of the bandits pulled out his gun and shot him. Archik watched from the marketplace as his uncle staggered into view and crumpled to the ground, dead.

The pogroms continued in Ostropolia throughout October, with attacks occurring every few days. In all, eleven Jews were reported slaughtered, dozens were wounded, and some seventy women were assaulted. Three of the eleven dead were Zabarkas. Ostropolia was decimated: many buildings had been totally destroyed and were uninhabitable. Lacking shelter and possessions, the Jews fled Ostropolia for Starokonstantinov, the largest town in the district.

Ada was in Odessa during the atrocities. But when she had a dream about her brother Louis being in tremendous peril, she decided to return home despite the risks. Stopping in Starokonstantinov on her way to Ostropolia, Ada heard that a rich Jew had been killed in the Ostropolia pogrom. She knew it had to be her father. She fainted on the spot.

When she arrived at her home, Ada hardly recognized her mother. Malke's face was red, swollen, and horribly disfigured where she had been shot. Ada learned that Louis had escaped and was hiding in a nearby town. Archik was holed up in the basement of a family friend, a local doctor, working as his assistant. She was shocked to hear that Rose had left Ostropolia, evidently for good.

Ada didn't know what to do. Bereft of her husband, a daughter, and a brother, with two sons in hiding and a daughter on her way to America, Malke made one of the most painful and selfless decisions a parent could contemplate: she urged Ada to leave Ostropolia for a better future. And so Ada departed for Warsaw to join Rose. While his sisters were in Warsaw arranging their passage, Louis was still in hiding, trying to decide what his next move should be.

Lilly Zabar's Meat Borscht and Flanken Soup

Edited and tested by Monita Buchwald

Borscht, meat or vegetarian, is the national dish of Ukraine, the predominant beet-growing region of Eastern Europe. Borscht incorporates long-lasting root vegetables—beets combined with the basic Slavic pairing of chopped onions and carrots. Flanken (Yiddish for short ribs) was among the cheapest cuts of meat in Eastern Europe and became popular fare for Shabbat and holiday meals. The Zabarkas and Teitelbaums found meat borscht and flanken soup especially comforting during the long cold winters in Ostropolia.

Meat Borscht

SERVES 6

INGREDIENTS

2 tablespoons vegetable oil
1 medium onion, diced
2 medium carrots, peeled and diced
4 medium beets, peeled and julienned
¼ cup tomato puree
1½ tablespoons red wine vinegar

4 cups beef stock (from flanken soup recipe, see following page)
1 medium potato, cut into ½-inch cubes
One-quarter small green cabbage, shredded and cut into 1-inch pieces (about 1 cup)
Kosher salt

Freshly ground black pepper
Cooked flanken meat, taken off
the bone and shredded into

small pieces (from 4 pounds
uncooked flanken on the bone;
see below)

DIRECTIONS

1. Heat the oil in a large pot over medium heat. Add the onion and sauté until soft and golden but not brown, about 10 minutes.
2. Add the carrots and sauté for 5 to 7 minutes.
3. Add the beets, tomato puree, and vinegar and cook for 5 minutes.
4. Add the stock and bring to a simmer. Cook, covered, for about 45 minutes, or until the vegetables are tender.
5. Add the potato and cabbage and cook for 15 to 20 minutes more. Season with salt and pepper to taste.
6. Add the meat until it is warmed through, about 5 minutes.

Flanken Soup

Flanken meat is cut across the ribs, not along the bone as for barbecue, and it should be marbled but not excessively fatty. This meat has a tendency to shrink after cooking, so figure about one pound, bones included, per person. The soup is better made the day before and refrigerated so that all the fat can be skimmed off and the broth used as a base for meat borscht.

MAKES 4 CUPS

INGREDIENTS

4 pounds flanken on the bone
2 medium onions, cut in half
2 celery stalks, cut in half
5 large carrots, peeled and cut in
half

2 to 3 garlic cloves (optional)
Kosher salt
Freshly ground black pepper
Half bunch each fresh parsley and
dill, washed

DIRECTIONS

1. Trim off the excess fat from the flanken and pour boiling water over the meat. Discard this water.

2. Put the meat in a soup pot and add fresh water just to cover the meat. Add the onions, celery, carrots, garlic if you like, and a generous amount of salt and pepper.

3. Simmer gently until the meat is fork-tender, 1 to 1½ hours, occasionally skimming the fat from the top.

4. In the last 10 minutes of cooking, add a handful of parsley and dill, either tied in a bunch with string (so that the little pieces don't float around) or wrapped in cheesecloth.

5. Remove the meat and reserve the carrots. Remove the vegetables from the broth and strain over the pot, pressing on the cooked vegetables to extract the juices. Slice the carrots for garnish. The meat can be served in the soup or as a second course, on or off the bone, with horseradish.

2

In Transit and Acclimating to America

IN 1920, MY GRANDMOTHER LILLY (SHE WAS STILL CALLED LEIKA THEN) joined the hundreds of Jews fleeing Ostropolia for America. "I came to this country all alone," she often told me plaintively. "I was only nineteen and weighed ninety pounds." The grandmother I knew was plump, and it was hard for me to imagine her as thin. Then again, Lilly did like to exaggerate for dramatic effect.

According to family lore, Lilly's parents sent her away because they were afraid their beautiful daughter would be molested in a pogrom. As a single girl, she could leave her life behind more easily than if she had been a married woman. The Teitelbaums thought it would be a temporary separation, until Russia's political turmoil and antisemitic persecution settled down.

So Lilly traveled to Warsaw, where she waited a year for her visa. Her friend Rose Zabarka joined her in the fall of 1920. Warsaw was a major European transit point for Jews seeking passage to the Americas. Many were part of a huge backlog of refugees who had been unable to leave Eastern Europe during World War I.

Despite the circumstances, Lilly and Rose's days were not all gloom and anxiety. With so many refugees their age waiting for visas, they socialized and took advantage of Warsaw's cultural offerings. Sometimes one of them would buy a ticket for the opera and then hand it off to a friend during intermission so that two could share the event at half the price. A professional photograph taken at the time shows Rose seated with four friends, all of them with bobbed hair and loose-fitting, short-sleeved dark dresses—Eastern European flappers.

In response to the thousands of Jews hoping to immigrate to

America, the Hebrew Immigrant Aid Society (HIAS) set up its Warsaw office in 1920 to assist in processing passports and visas. With the aid of the HIAS staff, Lilly and her fellow immigrants telegraphed their families abroad and waited for them to send money and affidavits of sponsorship. Some relatives remitted funds, and some didn't. If money didn't arrive, the refugees often had no option but to return to their hometowns.

Rose was the first to receive money and sponsorship, from her cousins Morris and Jacob (Gedalia) Leifer, who had a grocery store on East Twenty-Fifth Street in Manhattan. They were Malke's nephews, the sons of Rose's murdered uncle Lazar. Rose left for America in February 1921, with Lilly still waiting for her papers to come through. The two friends promised to meet up again in the New World.

Shortly thereafter, on March 12, Lilly departed for America from Danzig, the port nearest Warsaw, aboard the S.S. *Susquehanna,* with

Grandma Lilly, then Leika Teitelbaum (middle row, no. 7), among a group of Jewish refugees waiting to depart from Danzig in 1921.
(ERNA KEISEL/ZABAR FAMILY COLLECTION)

all the arrangements having been made by HIAS. In a photograph taken in Danzig with fellow Jewish refugees, she appears to accept her future with remarkable calm and gravitas.

The passage to America took exactly one month, and on April 12, 1921, Lilly arrived in Boston—all alone, as she frequently reminded me. What my grandmother did not tell me was that her maternal aunt and uncle Adia and David Toker (later Tucker) were also on the S.S. *Susquehanna,* a fact I discovered years later, when I obtained a copy of the ship's manifest. After landing, Lilly, her aunt, and her uncle traveled to the Tuckers' son's home in Newark, New Jersey. Six years older than Lilly and the proprietor of a confectionery store, Morris Tucker was one of my grandmother's favorite first cousins. Yet Lilly never mentioned her time in New Jersey. Her goal had always been New York City. An error on the ship's manifest that listed Morris's address as being in New York may have misled her into thinking she was headed there from the S.S. *Susquehanna.* She must have been quite disappointed, but as a penniless immigrant, she had no option but to live first in New Jersey with one cousin, and then in Philadelphia with other cousins. All told, Lilly would spend the next thirteen years working her way to a permanent residence in Manhattan.

In the Northern Liberties neighborhood of Philadelphia, Lilly stayed with the family of another maternal aunt, Jennie Stillman Rosen, relatives Lilly hadn't seen for a decade. Jennie's husband, Joseph, was a mason and plasterer who was successful enough to own the house where they lived, with three boarders and four grown children, including Lilly's favorite cousin, Bertha. Lilly was thrilled to be reunited with Bertha, a tall and vivacious twenty-one-year-old brunette, and the two chatted as if they had never been apart. Lilly was grateful that Bertha, who worked as a sewing machine operator at a ladies' "shirtwaist" (blouse) factory, was there to help her navigate her new American life. Someone who knew someone soon found Lilly a job at a nearby millinery factory. For long hours, she trimmed straw, felt, and wool hats with feathers. It was a period Lilly recalled as sheer drudgery.

When they weren't working, the Rosens shopped and kibitzed on North Marshall Street, the commercial hub of the neighborhood. Previously occupied by middle-class German Jews, this area now teemed with immigrants from Eastern Europe. The buildings on bustling Marshall Street were both the homes and shops of the storekeepers, a linear version of Ostropolia's outdoor bazaar. With only iceboxes to keep their food fresh—the ice was delivered daily by the iceman in his horse and wagon—residents of the Northern Liberties shopped at least once a day for their provisions. Husbands and wives manned their shops from dawn to dusk. Yiddish-speaking vendors sold produce from pushcarts. Chickens squawked and fish swam in tubs. The aromas of baking bread and spices permeated the air, competing with the smell of rotting fruits and vegetables and horse manure. Everyone *hondled*, or bargained, in a mixture of Russian, Polish, and Yiddish.

Lilly might have lived her whole life in Philadelphia had it not been for a *shidduch* (match) made within her family about a year after she arrived: Bertha became engaged to Abe Stillman, a first cousin to both Bertha and Lilly. (Marrying a close relative was common enough in the old country, but by the time my grandmother recounted this story to me, it was sufficiently frowned upon that she whispered that part of it.) Lilly was thrilled that Abe had a job in New York City as an auctioneer for Eichner Brothers on Lenox Avenue and 124th Street in Manhattan. "After Bertha married Abe Stillman," she later told me, "I moved to the Bronx with them. I wanted to be in New York City."

Bertha and Abe set up a household at 506 East 142nd Street, in the Mott Haven neighborhood of the Bronx. Their daughter Pearl was born in 1923, and Lilly moved in with the Stillmans on New Year's Day, 1924. The confined quarters did nothing to diminish the cousins' warm feelings for each other. My grandmother and Bertha would remain close for the rest of their lives.

By now, Lilly's friend Rose Zabarka and Rose's sister Ada had found their way to New York City as well, settling in upper Manhattan. Lilly soon resumed her friendship with the Zabarka girls, little guessing what a lifelong relationship it would turn out to be.

·   ·   ·

AS LILLY, ROSE, and Ada acclimated to their new lives in America, Louis was following a more circuitous route to New York. Soon after Ada left for Warsaw in the late fall of 1920, Louis decided to take a chance and left his hiding place to return to Ostropolia. He knew he was risking retribution from the local bandits he had threatened and the possibility of more pogroms to come. Upon his arrival, he found the even greater danger of Soviet military conscription awaiting him. Malke once again put her children's safety above her despair at losing another child. She urged Louis to join his sisters in Warsaw.

At this time, many Jews in the Pale of Settlement were paying Ukrainian peasants to take them across the border to Poland at night—risky for anyone, and particularly dangerous for males of draft age. But my grandfather had few options. Fearful for his future in the Soviet Union and enticed by the personal and financial opportunities in America, Louis decided to hazard being arrested and jailed to follow his sisters across the ocean. Malke hired an armed peasant to accompany and protect Louis on his clandestine journey out of the Soviet Union. To make sure the escort didn't just take the money and abandon or kill Louis, Malke arranged for him to be paid only after she received word from Louis that he had made it across the border. Louis arrived in Warsaw in the winter of 1921.

The timing was not in his favor. It was my grandfather's misfortune that the United States Congress passed the Emergency Quota Act on May 19, 1921, before he could obtain a visa from the American consulate. This law, championed by Americans who feared that the recent flood of immigrants from eastern and southern Europe would take away their jobs and/or reduce their wages, imposed limits on European immigration to America for the first time. It meant that Louis could not go to America as he had planned; according to the law's formula, the quota of Polish immigrants allowed into the United States that year had already been filled. His second choice was Canada, but he couldn't book his passage until the Canadian consulate received confirmation that a family member in Canada was willing to receive him.

While he waited in Warsaw for his application to be approved and his visa processed, Louis, along with other refugees, dictated in Yiddish the history of the recent pogroms in his town to a representative of the Joint Distribution Committee, the same organization that had rescued and transported Rose from Ostropolia to Warsaw. The JDC transcribed the accounts into typed documents and later translated them into English.

My grandfather never again discussed what he'd witnessed. I tried for years to put together the story of the pogrom that had propelled Louis to America, but my family knew only bits and pieces. It wasn't until 2013 that my uncle Saul received an email from a stranger in Montreal with Louis's dictated account attached. A man named Mattis Kovalenko had been looking in the JDC's digitized records for *his* great-grandfather, who had been the last rabbi in Ostropolia, when he found my grandfather's account in Yiddish. By a stroke of fate, I had finally gotten from my grandfather an answer to my questions.

After several months in Warsaw, Louis departed for Quebec in a third-class berth on the S.S. *Canada*. Upon his arrival on September 18, 1921, he declared that he was a twenty-year-old student who intended to be an electrician, that he had paid for the passage himself, and that he had the $250 required by the Canadian government for entry. The ship's manifest said his destination was a cousin named "Moris Eckenberg," whose address was 49 Wellington Avenue, Sherbrooke, Canada. Until I discovered this document, my father and my uncles never knew where my grandfather lived in Canada or who had sponsored him.

The Echenbergs were Louis's cousins by marriage. They were the first family to immigrate from Ostropolia to Sherbrooke in 1893 and were now prosperous merchants. Coincidentally, Louis arrived in Sherbrooke just in time for the wedding of his first cousin Jacob Leifer to Jacob's childhood sweetheart, Leah Echenberg, on September 27, 1921. It was Jacob and his brother Morris who had recently sponsored and taken in Louis's sisters Rose and Ada.

Jacob returned to New York with his bride, but my grandfather remained in Sherbrooke, surrounded by lakes, rivers, farmland, and forests, ninety-six miles from Montreal, in the Eastern Townships of

Quebec. Of the 275 Jews who made up 11 percent of Sherbrooke's population, 150 were originally from Ostropolia. And 75 of them were part of the extended Echenberg family. In Sherbrooke, Louis could communicate with his Ostropolia *landsleit* (Jews who come from the same town or village) in Yiddish, Russian, Hebrew, and Polish, but the majority of Sherbrooke's residents spoke French. The wealthy minority with whom the upwardly mobile Jews identified spoke English, and Louis picked up the language as he toiled as a lumberjack and in a bakery, where he schlepped heavy bags of flour that coated his back with powder as white as the Canadian snow. Employment wasn't easy to find.

Louis stayed in Canada for one year, almost to the day. He had always intended to join his relatives and friends in New York City when the time was right, and an economic downturn in Canada spurred his departure. Louis crossed over from Canada to the United States by car, arriving in Newport, Vermont, on September 15, 1922. As far as the Canadian and American authorities knew, he was a visitor looking forward to a pleasant automobile tour of America. But Louis, with little beyond a few words of newly learned, harshly accented English, had no intention of returning to Canada. First, he drove west to see what opportunities lay in Detroit, where he stayed with a cousin who was a successful grocer. But the burgeoning motor city didn't interest him, and he continued on to New York City to join Ada, Rose, and the Leifers. On the way, he found work washing cars in a gas station.

Compared with the newly arrived Zabarkas, Morris and Jacob Leifer were practically Yankees. Tall, robust, and reserved Morris was the opposite of his older brother Jacob, who was frail and bookish. They had left Ostropolia about a decade earlier to escape military conscription and were sent to Galveston, Texas, as part of an immigrant settlement program sponsored by several Jewish philanthropic organizations. The Galveston Movement was designed to disperse newly arrived Jews throughout the United States, to alleviate the terrible overcrowding in East Coast immigrant neighborhoods such as New York's Lower East Side. But Morris and Jacob were unhappy in Texas; they wanted to live with fellow immigrants from Ostropolia. And so they worked their way northeast, taking on a series of backbreaking shipping and construction jobs until they arrived in New York City in 1914.

Morris and Jacob had saved enough money to open a grocery store at 320 East Twenty-Fifth Street, on the north side of the street between First and Second Avenues. Their first cousin Pincus (Pinya) Zabarka was already in the grocery business, in a store around the corner at 311 East Twenty-Sixth Street. Born in 1891, stout Pinya was a son of Avrum and Feyga Zabarka, who shared Schlomo and Malke's two-family house in Ostropolia. In Russia, Pinya had loved

Louis Zabar, flanked by his adoring sisters
Rose and Ada, sometime in the early 1920s.
(ZABAR FAMILY COLLECTION)

music and played the violin, but now he worked seventeen-hour days, seven days a week, to support his wife and daughter.

Louis arrived in New York City in the fall of 1922, excited yet apprehensive. Dapper businessmen in three-piece suits and starched collars passed him on the unfamiliar streets, their hair slicked back and parted down the middle. Women looked sophisticated, too, with their cloche hats and slim-cut, drop-waist, knee-length dresses. Except for some basic English language skills, Louis had nothing to show for his year spent in Canada. He found it disheartening to be forced to rely on the kindness of his cousins, who housed him and helped him out financially, but at the same time he was thrilled to be reunited with his sisters, cousins, and friends.

New York City in the 1920s was a bustling Jazz Age metropolis teaming with people from many places—all of them trying to make a living. Louis was delighted when Morris and Jacob offered him a job at their store. The Leifers' grocery was one of several small shops located on the ground floors of the rowhouses and tenements that stretched across Twenty-Fifth Street. Inside, bushel baskets and wooden crates held whatever fruits and vegetables were in season. Behind dark wooden counters that lined the long, narrow shop, tall shelves were stacked with canned and packaged goods. At the back of the store were the bulk goods—coffee to be ground, sugar to be measured out, pickles to be plucked from their briny bath, wheels of cheese to be sliced. Burly in his big white apron, Morris stood behind one of the counters, waiting on the customers. Bookish Jacob was studying to be a pharmacist.

In 1920s America, almost anyone of modest means could become a grocer—even an immigrant with limited language skills. A shop, which sometimes came with an apartment right above it, could be rented inexpensively. A wholesaler might provide goods on credit. The overhead was low because it was the owner and his family who worked twelve to fourteen hours a day to provide personal service to neighborhood shoppers.

Louis worked in the grocery all day and slept in a storage room behind the store at night. The noisy elevated train that ran up and down Second Avenue shook the buildings and left them and the streets in perpetual shadow. It was quite a different life from the one Louis had enjoyed in Ostropolia. Here in New York the son of Schlomo Zabarka—a wealthy merchant who once sold lumber, produce, and other goods throughout Ukraine—now stacked boxes and swept the sawdust off the floor of his cousins' store. His goal was to make enough money to start his own business and send funds to his mother and siblings, who were now living in poverty in Ostropolia. He was eager to learn whatever he could from Morris and Jacob, accompanying them to buy fruits and vegetables at the wholesale markets, noting how much they bought and from whom.

On one of his days off, Louis went to Coney Island and bought a ticket to ride the huge Ferris wheel. Sensing that Louis was newly arrived to America, the operator decided to use him to drum up business—by stopping the wheel when he'd reached the top and leaving him there for an hour in the hot sun. Louis was furious. The incident left him all the more determined to show the world that he was no ignorant greenhorn.

In the evenings, Louis enjoyed getting together with his sisters and other relatives and friends from Ostropolia. One evening, someone—most likely Rose—brought along Leika Teitelbaum, who now called herself Lillian and lived in the Bronx. Of course, Louis immediately recognized Lilly—now with a fashionable light brown bob—as the pretty girl with whom he would share the apples he brought to school back in Ostropolia.

Lilly envied Louis for being in Manhattan—despite the fact that he lived in a storage room. But Louis didn't plan to stay with his cousins forever. He had learned the ropes from Morris and Jacob and after a couple of years with them felt that he was ready to make his own way. In his first attempt at independence, Louis sold fruits and vegetables in Brooklyn, from a stall in one of the covered markets beneath the Brooklyn Bridge. It was one of the more than fifty open-air markets then operating in the city. Selling produce from a pushcart was the lowest rung on the retail food ladder. One didn't need much capital or much knowledge of English to do this. Louis was embarrassed for his family to see him there.

By 1925, Louis had earned enough to move to an area of Brooklyn between Brownsville and Bedford-Stuyvesant. There he embarked on a series of brief partnerships in small mom-and-pop fruit and vegetable stores. By now, Louis was seriously courting Lilly. Being together was like going home to Ostropolia, and this suited both of them. Louis had his two sisters to keep him company, but Lilly had left her immediate family behind and often felt lonely. Spending time with the Zabarkas and the Leifers made her feel closer to home. She and Louis didn't have to explain their backgrounds or family histories to each other. They had the same taste in food and enjoyed the same leisure activities. They both drank their hot tea from tall glasses with a sugar cube clenched between their front teeth, and they loved competing vigorously at canasta and gin rummy. They both spoke the languages of Ostropolia. (Lilly may have had an additional reason for her attraction to Louis. One cousin told me that she was at the time on the rebound from an unsuccessful love affair.) Louis was not a man of means, but in Lilly's estimation he appeared to be a good bet: ambitious, energetic, and virile.

Most likely to commemorate their engagement, Louis and Lilly headed one day to Waterman's, photographers who were located at 298 Willis Avenue in Mott Haven, not far from the Bronx Terminal Market (a state-of-the-art wholesale food facility) and the recently opened Yankee Stadium. In the photograph they had taken there, my grandparents appear happy and optimistic, ready to embark on a life together. They both look straight at the camera, smiling slightly as they lean into each other.

On Monday, May 2, 1927, Louis Zabar, as he now called himself, and Lillian Teitelbaum got married in an apartment on South Second Street in Williamsburg, Brooklyn. Louis was twenty-six and Lilly was twenty-four, but she had already shaved two years off her age on the marriage certificate, which stated that she was twenty-two. From then on, my grandmother's true age remained a state secret. As a child, I once heard her claim to be several years younger than she actually was, prompting Aunt Ada to scoff, "Lilly, don't be ridiculous! I know exactly how old you are. We grew up together in Ostropolia."

On February 1, 1928, half a year into their marriage and in her second trimester of pregnancy, Lilly filed a petition to become a naturalized citizen. She had begun the process several years earlier

*Louis and Lilly at about the time of
their marriage in 1927.* (WATERMAN'S
PHOTOGRAPHERS/ZABAR FAMILY COLLECTION)

in the Bronx, but her pregnancy must have compelled her to finish it up and stake a permanent hold in America. My grandmother was a perpetual worrywart under the best of circumstances, and because Louis was in America illegally and therefore unable to file for citizenship, she must have been particularly eager to become a citizen herself as she faced the impending birth of her child.

Lilly and Louis's first child, my uncle Saul, was born on June 4, 1928. My grandparents chose a name beginning with *S* in memory of my slain great-grandfather Schlomo. (Eventually, the first sons of all of Schlomo's children were given names beginning with *S*.) On July 3, a month after Saul's birth and a day before Independence Day, Lillian Zabar swore an oath of allegiance to the United States of America in Brooklyn federal court. She was officially a

U.S. citizen. Despite being under oath, she also managed to whittle another year off her age.

After Saul's birth, my grandparents made several moves within Brooklyn in their quest for success in the retail fruit and vegetable business. The first stop was a produce shop at 284 Brighton Beach Avenue, which was on a low-rise commercial strip facing the elevated BMT train tracks. Louis and Lilly lived around the corner at 3101 Lakeland Place (now Brighton Second Street), in an early-twentieth-century brick, stucco, and wood Tudor-style apartment building that was just a block from the spacious, sandy beach that faced the Atlantic Ocean.

Grandly named after the English seaside resort, Brighton Beach had been developed as a resort community in the late nineteenth century, next to Coney Island. By the time the Zabars arrived in the 1920s, it had begun to transform itself into a pleasant seaside residential neighborhood. The construction of the BMT subway line linking Brighton Beach to Manhattan encouraged many Jews to move there from Brownsville, East New York, and the Lower East Side.

Brighton Beach was a little Russia-by-the-Sea when Louis and Lilly lived there, just as it is today. Everyone spoke Yiddish or Russian. My grandmother worked side by side with my grandfather in their store, piling the apples into an attractive pyramid or ringing up potatoes at the cash register. They took turns returning to the apartment to check on Saul and the maid who took care of him, to have lunch, or to just take a break during the long days and catch a breeze from the ocean. They had little, but they were optimistic. With luck and hard work, they were sure they could secure a comfortable life and their small piece of the American dream. But their luck didn't hold, as the stock market crash on October 29, 1929, heralded the onset of what became known as the Great Depression. The women of Brighton Beach—always tight with a penny—tightened their purse strings even more. The local businesses struggled to stay afloat.

As my grandmother told the story, one day when Louis was out, some men entered the store and watched as Lilly waited on the customers. They questioned her about the store's traffic and about the customers' tastes in produce. They appeared to be interested in the business, so Lilly presented it in the best possible light. By the time Louis returned, she had sold the store to these complete strangers.

My grandmother's account is charming but, alas, untrue—or at least highly exaggerated. My research revealed that the purchaser of the store was the Zion Brighton Public Market. Abraham Zion, an immigrant from Shepetowka, Russia, owned a number of fruit and vegetable stores in Brooklyn. According to family lore, Louis had worked for Zion before he had his own business, and Zion remained a mentor, close business colleague, and friend.

By the summer of 1931, Louis had managed to move a few miles closer to Manhattan—which was where Lilly still dreamed of living. His new fruit and vegetable store was in Flatbush, at 1911 Kings Highway. Not an individual mom-and-pop operation, this store was part of a group of markets in Brooklyn called Confidence, an association of independent purveyors grouped under a brand-name umbrella. Louis shared the space with the Confidence meat department. Right next door, at 1909 Kings Highway, was the Confidence fish market.

By 1933, Louis M. Zabar was the president and treasurer of the Confidence Fruit and Vegetable Market, Inc. That same year, the Zabar family—which now also included my father, Stanley Jerome, who had been born on August 19, 1932—moved from Brighton Beach to a brick apartment house at 2642 Ocean Avenue in Flatbush, several blocks from Louis's store.

Louis and Lilly spent four years as the proprietors of the Confidence Fruit and Vegetable Market. During that period, my grandfather developed an uncomfortable, itchy rash on his arms and hands—an allergic reaction to handling fruit and vegetable skins. The rash never stopped Louis from working, and as he toiled, he noticed that only one thing helped: when he plunged his hands and arms in a barrel of pickled herring, the brine soothed his rash. But Louis didn't want to live in a perpetual state of skin irritation and realized he would have to find some other food items to sell.

He soon did, and the rest is history.

Lilly Zabar's Chicken Soup with Matzoh Balls (Knaidlach)

Edited and tested by Monita Buchwald

Chicken soup is the perfect balm for homesickness as well as for physical ailments. While Louis, Ada, Rose, and Lilly were acclimating to their new country, chicken soup with matzoh balls evoked memories of the childhood warmth and security that had been provided by their mothers in Ostropolia. Lilly served her chicken soup at Friday-night Shabbat dinner and on Jewish holidays. Her matzoh balls were light as a feather and her boiled chicken so moist and tender it fell off the bone. First, she served the soup and matzoh balls and then the chicken on the bone in quarters—or in eighths, if it was a large chicken. These two courses were a filling meal. Though some people shred the chicken into the soup, Grandma Lilly never did.

Chicken Soup

MAKES 2 QUARTS; SERVES 8

INGREDIENTS

One 4- to 5-pound chicken, cut into quarters, cleaned and washed, any visible fat removed with a small paring knife and saved for schmaltz (page 170)

2 celery stalks, cut into quarters
1 large onion, cut into quarters
2 to 3 large carrots, peeled and cut in half
2-inch piece of fresh ginger

2 garlic cloves
Kosher salt
Freshly ground black pepper
Small bunch fresh parsley (tied
with string)

Small bunch fresh dill (tied with
string)
Bouillon cube (optional)

DIRECTIONS

1. Place the chicken in a large soup pot. Pour boiling water over the chicken to cover. Let stand for 5 minutes and then drain the water.
2. Add cold water just to cover the chicken. Add the celery, onion, carrots, ginger, and garlic. Season with salt and pepper to taste.
3. Simmer until the chicken is tender, about 1 hour. Add the parsley and dill during last 20 minutes of cooking. If you prefer the chicken more done, almost falling off the bone, continue cooking to your preference. Taste, adding a bouillon cube if desired.
4. Remove the chicken and carrots. Strain the soup, mashing the juices of the vegetables through the strainer. Let cool, chill, and then skim the fat.
5. To serve, add the chicken pieces back into the strained broth. Gently reheat. Cut the carrots into disks to garnish the soup.

Matzoh Balls (Knaidlach)

MAKES ABOUT 18 MATZOH BALLS

INGREDIENTS

4 large eggs
¼ cup schmaltz (rendered chicken
fat), coconut oil, or vegetable oil
¼ cup seltzer, chicken stock, or
vegetable stock
2 tablespoons freshly grated
ginger

2 tablespoons finely chopped fresh
parsley, dill, or cilantro
2 teaspoons kosher salt, plus
more for cooking
Freshly ground black pepper
1 cup matzoh meal

DIRECTIONS

1. Combine the eggs, schmaltz, seltzer, ginger, and parsley in a large bowl. Season with the 2 teaspoons salt and a few grinds of pepper. Gently mix with a whisk or spoon.

2. Add the matzoh meal ⅓ cup at a time. Stir to wet and absorb all the matzoh meal. (If the matzoh meal is added all at once, the mixture will turn to cement.) The mixture will be a bit loose but firmer after it chills.

3. Cover and refrigerate until chilled, about 3 hours or overnight.

4. To shape and cook the matzoh balls, fill a wide deep pan with lightly salted water and bring to a boil. With wet hands, take some of the mixture and mold it into a ball the size of a walnut. Gently drop the ball into the boiling water. Repeat until all of the mixture is used.

5. Cover the pan, reduce the heat to a lively simmer, and cook the matzoh balls for about 50 minutes. If desired, the cooked matzoh balls can be transferred to chicken or vegetable soup and served immediately. Alternatively, they may be placed on a baking sheet and frozen, then transferred to a freezer bag and kept frozen until a few hours before serving. Reheat in chicken or vegetable soup or broth.

3

The Beginning of Zabar's

IN THE AUTUMN OF 1934, MY GRANDFATHER HAD A FATEFUL CONVER-sation with a man named Charlie Raffa. A gregarious fellow with a thick Italian accent, Charlie owned the Ideal Fixture Company, which sold supermarket equipment to fellow immigrant entrepreneurs. Affectionately dubbed "Charlie Ideal" by his customers, he was known for providing them with affordable payment terms. (Four decades later, he would become even better known as Matilda Cuomo's father and Governor Mario Cuomo's father-in-law.) Charlie told Louis about an available retail space on the Upper West Side of Manhattan.

The space Charlie recommended was in the Crystal Pure Food Market, at 2249 Broadway, between West Eightieth and Eighty-First Streets. (The venue actually encompassed two buildings, 2249 and 2247 Broadway.) It was a good location for a retail store. Even though America was in the depths of the Great Depression, the Upper West Side was still a relatively prosperous residential neighborhood. It was also largely Jewish, as many of its residents had migrated there from the teeming Lower East Side when they became more successful. On weekends, men in bespoke suits and women in furs paraded up and down Broadway with their well-dressed children, exchanging greetings. Newly arrived German Jews, fleeing Hitler's Third Reich, could be found having coffee or tea at Steinberg's Dairy Restaurant or the Éclair pastry shop.

This stretch of upper Broadway was already a hub of food retailers and restaurants such as the Great Atlantic & Pacific Tea Company (a grocery store that eventually grew into the iconic A&P supermarket chain), the Little Tip Toe Inn, and the Sherman Cafeteria. Across the street stood the Dubowy Bakery and Dairy Restaurant, the Broadway Cafeteria, and the G&M Pastry Shop.

Louis and Lilly rented a counter in the Crystal Pure Food Market and moved their operation to the new space in the fall of 1934. The entire store encompassed 2,500 square feet on the street level of a five-story Italianate structure (the northernmost section of the five buildings that make up Zabar's today). Sawdust covered the wooden floors and the air was rich with the aromas of smoked salmon, delicatessen meats, and tangy pickled vegetables. Because of Louis's skin allergy to fresh fruits and vegetables, they had switched to selling more lucrative and nonallergenic appetizing and delicatessen.

Three other shopkeepers occupied space in the Crystal Market and, just like Louis, they were all ambitious tradesmen from immigrant families. On the market's north side, Jackie Sloan sold fruits and vegetables. Jackie was a relative of Max Sloan, who owned several produce shops on upper Broadway called the Orange Grove and eventually founded the Sloan's Supermarket chain. Abraham J. Dubin, a member of the Daitch Crystal Dairies family, owned and managed the Crystal Market and also sold milk, butter, cheese, and eggs in the front of the store. Toward the back of the space, butcher Sigmund Rosengarten sold fresh meat and fish. Rosengarten later founded the Shopwell Supermarket chain in Westchester County. (In 1955, the two businesses, by then both significant supermarket chains in the greater New York region, merged to become Daitch Shopwell. In the 1980s, the chain morphed once more, into The Food Emporium.)

When my grandparents opened their store on the Upper West Side, they decided to call it Zabar's, and that has been its name ever since. For the first two years, Louis listed his business in the telephone directory as a delicatessen, but then he changed it to "appetizer." It stayed that way for the next three years.

The initial, late-nineteenth- and early-twentieth-century distinction between a delicatessen (which sold cured and prepared meat, such as pastrami, corned beef, tongue, salami, hot dogs, roast beef, brisket, and chopped liver) and an appetizing store (which sold smoked, cured, and pickled fish, including salmon, lox, herring, and whitefish, as well as cheese, butter, and bagels) was created for religious reasons. Kosher-keeping customers would not purchase meat and dairy products from the same store because knives that sliced pastrami could not also be used to cut Swiss cheese, and the platters that held deli meat could not later be used for herring in cream sauce. But these distinctions were less meaningful to my grandparents, who kept kosher only at home, and from the get-go Zabar's advertised itself as a "kosher-style" store. This was an unofficial, flexible term that generally meant that meat and dairy products were sold in the same store, were not prepared separately, and were not produced under rabbinical supervision. But—at least in the early years—you weren't going to find in Zabar's such resoundingly nonkosher items as ham, bacon, and lobster. Zabar's customers—the upper-middle-class Jews who had moved into those elegant apartment buildings on Central Park West, West End Avenue, and Riverside Drive, and who did not keep kosher themselves—were fine with all this. Just as my great-grandparents Schlomo and Malke were less traditionally observant than their parents in their choices of attire and education for their children, so Louis and Lilly adapted their business to modern American Jewish practices.

After many years of selling fruits and vegetables, my grandfather had become a perfectionist about the quality of his goods. For this new venture, Louis would sample deli meats and fish from various purveyors before he would commit to doing business with those suppliers. To taste fish, Louis would tour dozens of local smokehouses, large and small, mostly in Brooklyn and Queens. He was notorious among the wholesalers for rejecting more than he accepted. His retail mantra was simple: the highest quality at the lowest price.

Cured and smoked fish were popular in observant Jewish homes because they are pareve, neither meat nor dairy, and can be eaten with either, according to Jewish law. Salmon, prepared in a variety of ways, became a Zabar's mainstay. Lox, derived from the Yiddish version of the German word for salmon, *lachs*, was soaked in a cold salt brine for three to six months and then briefly washed to remove excess salt. Lox was not smoked or cooked; the salt brine preserved the fish. American Jews of Eastern European ancestry ate primarily lox until the mid-twentieth century, when many people decided that lox was too salty and switched to Nova Scotia–style smoked salmon, or "novie," instead. (Customers often still referred to novie as lox.)

Nova Scotia salmon, originally only from Canada, was placed in tubs of brine containing salt and brown sugar and soaked in a cold room for about a week. Then the salmon was removed from the brine and smoked for eighteen to twenty-four hours at a temperature ranging from 70 to 76 degrees Fahrenheit, in a process called cold smoking.

Smoked Scotch salmon is wild salmon from Scotland, dry-cured with salt and cold-smoked in the British tradition. It has a subtler, less salty flavor and less oily texture than novie. Because of its milder flavor, smoked Scotch salmon is eaten with butter or crème fraîche on rye or sourdough bread rather than with cream cheese and bagels (a combination that originated in the 1930s). Until then, cured and smoked fish was traditionally consumed with butter on dark pumpernickel or rye bread.

Another type of smoked salmon sold at Zabar's is baked or "kippered" salmon, which is hot-smoked starting at 100 degrees Fahrenheit and then increased to 200 degrees over six to eight hours, producing a moist cooked fish.

To be near their new enterprise, Louis, Lilly, Saul, and Stanley moved from Brooklyn to an apartment in a five-story walk-up at 175 West Eighty-First Street, on the northeast corner of Amsterdam Avenue, just a block east of their store. Although it wasn't a fancy building, for my grandmother, who had yearned to be in Manhattan, it was a dream fulfilled. A little more than a year later, they moved down the street, to 204 West Eighty-First Street, a slightly nicer building that actually had an elevator. Slowly but surely, my grandparents were inching their way toward better lives.

President Franklin Roosevelt's New Deal programs had effectively stimulated the nation's recovery from the Great Depression. Zabar's, along with other retailers, was doing well. In the fall of 1938, with their business flourishing, the Zabars moved one last time, to a fifth-floor apartment at 219 West Eighty-First Street, a

*Saul, Louis, Stanley, and Lilly, circa 1938,
the year they moved to 219 West Eighty-First
Street.* (ZABAR FAMILY COLLECTION)

grand, twelve-story, white-brick-and-limestone building just half a block away from the store. Their new apartment—which would nowadays be described as a classic six—featured a living room, a dining room, two full bedrooms, a bathroom, a kitchen, and an adjacent "maid's room" with bathroom, which was occupied by their newly acquired maid, Matilda. In addition to an elevator, the new apartment boasted another unmistakable indicator that the Zabars were now part of New York's upper middle class: a doorman.

Saul and Stanley experienced the full spectrum of joys and challenges of growing up on the Upper West Side in the 1930s. The buildings on Amsterdam and Columbus Avenues and on the side streets between them were for the most part utilitarian structures, such as garages and stables, or tenements occupied by the service people who supported the well-heeled residents on the posher avenues to the east and west—Central Park West, West End Avenue, and Riverside Drive. Jewish kids walking on those dingier blocks had to be on the lookout for the local Irish and Italian tough kids, who were always spoiling for a fight. Ever the problem solver, my father made a point of becoming friends with an older boy who would protect him.

Saul and Stanley walked to school at P.S. 9 on Eighty-Second Street and West End Avenue, one block west of their apartment and Zabar's. Now a designated New York City landmark, the school is a handsome Dutch Revival building with pale ocher brick and a stepped roof, designed by the acclaimed public-school architect Charles B. J. Snyder. But just as my father was acclimating to first grade, he developed a mastoid infection behind his left ear that required an operation and convalescence at home. He missed so much school, he didn't learn to read and had to redo his first semester. To add insult to injury, Saul, a fourth grader, delighted in reminding anyone who'd listen that his brother, Stanley, had been left back.

My father made it to second grade eventually, where he was so popular with the girls that to this day the neighborhood women fondly reminisce about their time as Stanley's classmate. The late Emily Mason, who became a renowned artist, remembered Stanley welcoming her into the class when she was the new girl; this was backed up by Ellen Alpert Zuckerman, who told me her parents owned the Park Memorial Funeral Home and swore that my father was the kindest boy in second grade.

In those days, young children had more freedom to roam about the Upper West Side on their own than they do today. When they weren't in school or doing assigned research at the St. Agnes branch of the New York Public Library on Amsterdam Avenue, Saul and Stanley strolled up and down Broadway with their friends and cousins, or played in Riverside and Central Parks. Sometimes they went to the American Museum of Natural History. On Saturdays, my grandmother parked them at the RKO Keith's movie theater across the street from Zabar's, to see a double feature plus cartoon and

Looking north on Broadway from Seventy-Ninth Street, 1957. Zabar's is in
the Tudor-style building on the corner of Broadway and Eightieth Street.
Across the street is a former RKO movie theater that became the CBS
Studio 72 television studio in 1954 (it's now a Staples). Just north of the
theater was the Zabar family residence, at 219 West Eighty-First Street.
(BRIAN MERLIS/OLD NYC PHOTOS)

newsreel. At that time, New York City required movie theaters to
have a children's section for youngsters under age sixteen, which
was monitored by a flashlight-wielding matron. While the audi-
torium portion in the rear of the building was demolished years
ago, the handsome white terra-cotta front, with its large arched
windows, still graces Broadway, now as a branch of Staples.

Saul and Stanley also found their own particular advantage to
living in a building that did not face busy Broadway: they could
use relatively quiet West Eighty-First Street as their personal urban
playground. One of their favorite games was Johnny-on-the-Pony,
in which the boys and their friends climbed on top of one another
until they were piled so high they toppled down to the ground like
human pickup sticks.

If they forgot the key to their apartment, they could always walk
a half block over to the store where their parents were working,
but the boys came up with a much more creative approach. They'd
knock on their next-door neighbor's door, and from the neighbor's
balcony they could shimmy onto their own balcony and then slip

into their apartment through an open window. My grandparents never knew about this innovation, which was probably for the best.

If I had to guess, I'd suspect that Saul was the architect of the balcony incursions. Saul is a brilliant, energetic rebel who has always leapt into life—sometimes without regard for the consequences for himself or others. My father, on the other hand, is a rule follower, a cautious and studious planner. Each son took after some aspect of their father. Saul had Louis's volatile risk-taker personality, and Stanley embodied his perseverance, his determination to succeed, and his devotion and loyalty to family.

Even regular family meals demonstrated their contrasting personalities. My father liked to eat carefully and methodically—first his lamb chop, then his peas, then his mashed potatoes. For dessert, he'd work through the canned fruit cocktail the same way, consuming first the cubed pears, then the peaches, then the apples, then the grapes, all the while saving the bright red cherry—his favorite—for last. But Saul loved nothing more than to wait until just before Stanley was done to swoop up the cherry from Stanley's bowl with his spoon and pop it into his mouth. Even as an adult, Saul has a habit of absentmindedly reaching over to someone else's plate; for Saul's seventy-fifth birthday, my father gave him a huge retractable wooden fork that could extend several feet.

When not eating at home, one of their frequent lunch spots was Steinberg's Dairy Restaurant, a few doors up from their apartment building. One day, my father was in the mood for Steinberg's blueberry blintzes, thin crepe-like pancakes filled with sweetened farmer cheese and topped with sour cream or fruit sauce. The waiter was standing beside their table with his back to them, talking to another waiter and ignoring my father's attempts to get his attention. My uncle tried next, writing BLUEBERRY BLINTZES with a blue ballpoint pen on the waiter's starched white cuff, but the waiter continued to ignore them. Fed up, my uncle yelled, "WAITER! MY BROTHER WANTS BLUEBERRY BLINTZES!" The waiter turned around, held up his cuff, and in the Yiddish-accented tones of a Jewish vaudeville comic calmly replied, "Sir, I already hef deh order." Every now and then, Saul took his brother's side.

Other times, my father suffered the indirect consequences of his brother's misbehavior. My grandfather had promised to take Saul and Stanley to Coney Island on his day off. The boys looked forward to the trip all week long. Then, on the morning of the outing, Saul did something that angered Louis—not a rare occurrence, as Saul had a habit of irritating Louis by doing things like frittering away his allowance on candy. For this particular infraction, the response was swift. "I'm *not* taking you boys out this afternoon!" Louis roared. "And, Saul, you misbehave one more time and we'll send you to military school!" My uncle was never sent to military school—but my father didn't get to go to Coney Island that day, either. Years later, my father told me he realized Saul's punishment was probably just an excuse. My grandfather preferred to spend his limited free time playing cards with his friends.

Louis devoted himself to Zabar's, but he was always on the lookout for new developments in the food industry. The innovative, time-saving concept of self-service, first introduced in the 1910s, now drew his attention. Self-service grocery stores that sold packaged dry goods such as coffee, sugar, and flour; canned goods; prepackaged perishable meats; and fresh produce began proliferating in the 1920s, and the first true supermarkets started to appear in 1930. More quickly followed. Louis took notice of this intimidating new competitor. The supermarkets (some of them chain stores) did not offer the counter service that Zabar's did, but the spacious, well-stocked stores were a convenient and inexpensive way to shop. In the summer of 1939, Louis hedged his bets and opened a grocery store a few blocks away. He called it the King Stanley Self-Service Center. (The name was most likely inspired by the first American supermarket, King Kullen, which Michael J. Cullen opened in 1930, in a six-thousand-square-foot garage in Jamaica, Queens.) The King Stanley occupied the ground floor of 302 Columbus Avenue, between Seventy-Fourth and Seventy-Fifth Streets, a five-story nineteenth-century redbrick building with a black metal cornice on which a sign reading THE J.M. HORTON ICE CREAM COMPANY appeared (it's still visible today).

During the same summer of 1939, Abraham Dubin, Louis's landlord, decided to sell his dairy business; his employees were agitating for unionization and he wanted no part of it. By this point, my grandfather had made enough money to enable him to take over Dubin's lease of the market space in 2249 Broadway and greatly expand his own store. A sign over the entrance proudly proclaimed ZABAR'S FOOD MARKET, which now offered its customers a much wider array of products, including a number of unquestionably *traif* items such as pork and sturgeon. And Louis changed the telephone directory listing of the business yet again—to Zabar's Grocery & Delicatessen—to reflect his expanded selection of merchandise.

America's recovery from the Great Depression had been accelerated by a defense industry that, as of 1941, was allowed to sell armaments to countries that were officially at war with Germany. Now that people had more money in their pockets, business at Zabar's boomed accordingly. In the summer of 1940, only a year after taking over the lease on the market space at 2249 Broadway, Louis decided to move Zabar's two doors south. The other vendors stayed next door at 2247 Broadway, but Zabar's was now located at 2245 Broadway. To this day, it remains Zabar's official address.

This store, the former address of the Sherman Cafeteria, had new, refrigerated display windows that faced out on Broadway, and Louis used them as a bright, tempting stage piled high with smoked fish, deli meats, and sausages to seduce the thousands of strolling passersby each day. When customers entered the new Zabar's premises, they would see the appetizing counter on one side and the dairy department—milk, butter, eggs, and cheese—on the other. Farther back were the meats—pot roast, roast beef, corned beef, pastrami, hot dogs—and items such as pickles, sauerkraut, and canned goods.

Sundays were the busiest times at Zabar's, packed with shoppers stocking up for a traditional family brunch of appetizing. In the oral history *It Happened in Manhattan* by Myrna Katz Frommer and Harvey Frommer, a Zabar's customer named Jane Bevans described being enthralled by the long and glistening smoked fish counter, behind which my grandfather stood, taking orders. When he asked young Jane, "Vadaya vant, honey?" she always asked for "stomach salmon" rather than "belly lox," a term her grandmother had deemed uncouth. "Oh, you're Mrs. Apt's granddaughter," he would say. "I recognize your voice; I recognize the 'stomach salmon.' Anything gelse?"

Shoppers and store employees had to hustle on Sundays, because for hundreds of years New York State blue laws banned the operation of many businesses on the Christian day of rest and limited the hours of operation of numerous others: Zabar's could be open on Sundays only from 9:00 a.m. to 11:00 a.m. and from 4:00 p.m. to 7:00 p.m. The bifurcated working hours made Sunday staff hard to find, so Louis and Lilly conscripted family members to work on Sundays (and also to ignore the blue laws). Luckily, Ada and her husband, Jack Wagner, had followed Ada's beloved Louis to the Upper West Side from Seagate, Brooklyn. Ada managed the cash register and Jack, a chemical engineer by training, manned the appetizing counter. Their teenage son, Steve, the eldest of the Zabar cousins and Louis's favorite nephew, also came in to help, as did his sister, Anna May.

Saul and my father were still youngsters then, but they pitched in on Sundays, too. Because Louis kept the store open beyond permissible hours, one of Saul's duties was serving as a lookout for police officers who patrolled in search of blue-law violators. Other times, he tended the dairy counter, selling sour cream and sweet cream by the dipper and cutting thick slices from blocks of butter. Directly behind him, the refrigerated display case held Swiss, American, Muenster, and Cheddar cheese. The store's celebrated house brand of coffee—King Saul—was named after my uncle, who shared the name with the first king of Israel.

Those early years in the new space were exciting and prosperous. Zabar's soon developed an extensive charge account and delivery trade that counted aficionados such as George Gershwin, Fanny Brice, and Babe Ruth among its customers. The employees were as colorful as the clientele. One of Zabar's most vivid characters was Pearl Watman, the daughter of Lilly's beloved cousins Bertha and Abe Stillman. Gravel-voiced Pearl was an unforgettable presence: she was large and vivacious, with a striking olive complexion, a prominent nose, and black hair swept into a glamorous French twist. By the time she retired in 1986 at age sixty-six, Pearl had worked as the bookkeeper and office controller at Zabar's for forty-four years (save for a two-year wartime stint in a Rosie the Riveter–type job at the Brooklyn Navy Yard). One time, after a tooth extraction, Pearl went home to recuperate, but Louis, panicked by her absence, ordered her to return to the office. She did, reluctantly, with a wad of blood-stained cotton still stuffed in her swollen cheek. Nevertheless, Pearl was so fond of her demanding boss that a year after his death, she named her baby daughter Joy Lynne—the *L* in Lynne in memory of Louis.

Another favorite employee was Aaron Klein, a Russian Jewish immigrant who had worked for Louis in both Brooklyn and Manhattan. Aaron was like an older son to Louis. (When Saul and Stanley wanted to go to the 1939 New York World's Fair in Queens, a busy Louis asked Aaron to take them.) Aaron would eventually become a partner in a number of Louis's businesses. A charming extrovert with a flair for theater and display, Aaron had a lively, outgoing nature that complemented Louis's diligence. Aaron could sell you anything—whether you needed it or not. He even sold Louis on his younger cousin Murray Klein, a World War II refugee who became an employee, and later, a partner at Zabar's. Warm, witty, and wise, Aaron would evolve into a mentor for Saul, Stanley, and Murray after Louis's untimely death in 1950.

My grandmother also worked in the store. A woman of many talents, Lilly had a particular aptitude for law enforcement, serving as Zabar's one-woman security force. If she spotted someone stuffing a can of peas or a bag of coffee into his jacket, Lilly had no qualms about confronting the person and giving him a good talking-to. Rarely did she need to summon the authorities.

When she wasn't policing the store, Lilly sometimes labored in the tiny, narrow kitchen on the second floor, alongside a marvelous Black cook named Marie. Marie's gastronomic talents leaned toward all-American favorites, such as roast beef and her hand-peeled potato salad. Lilly, on the other hand, focused on Jewish cuisine, from chopped liver to noodle kugel. For Passover, Marie assisted Lilly in preparing Lilly's mother's gefilte fish, oval-shaped patties of poached ground fish served on Shabbat and holidays. For hours, Lilly and Marie would stand side by side, preparing the fish stock and mixing the ground whitefish, yellow pike, and carp with matzoh meal, onions, and eggs. The carp, Lilly maintained, added an earthy flavor. (Jews from Ukraine like their gefilte fish savory, not sweetened with sugar as it is in Poland.) Zabar's uses Grandma Lilly's gefilte fish recipe to this day.

Passover at the store was always special. The staff covered the wood shelves in white paper and displayed every conceivable Passover item, from Manischewitz matzoh and grape juice to Rokeach soap and silver polish. Pearl and others scribbled delivery orders as they cascaded into the store; Shorty, the deliveryman and Zabar's only non-Jewish employee until the mid-1940s, made his rounds with a pushcart. On the first night of Passover, Zabar's always closed early (and still does) so that everyone could hurry home before sundown for the family seder.

At their own seder, Louis and Lilly gathered relatives and friends around a long table capable of seating twenty-five. Haggadah in hand, Louis conducted the service before the meal, leading the reading, praying, and singing in Hebrew, while Stanley and Saul sat impatiently with their cousins. They couldn't wait to eat Lilly's homemade gefilte fish topped with hand-grated horseradish that burned their eyes and cleared their sinuses, the chicken soup with pillowy matzoh balls, and the boiled chicken that fell off the bone in rich, silky threads. For the children, the seder was a long, dull service. For Louis and Lilly, it was a celebration of a personal exodus from religious persecution in the Old World to America—their promised land of freedom and dignity.

Louis's work ethic had always been formidable. He arrived at the store each day at dawn and returned home just for a quick dinner. Though he often fell asleep on the living room rug after eating, as soon as he woke up, he'd return to the store and work until they closed at midnight. The only way he could take some time off and relax was by removing himself—literally—from the businesses. For several years starting in 1939, when Saul was eleven and Stanley seven, my grandparents spent the summer in a rented house in a rural residential community in northern Westchester. Mohegan Colony was only a fifty-minute drive from Manhattan, but with its pine trees and lake, the terrain was similar to Ostropolia. Eventually, in 1943, Louis and Lilly stopped renting in Mohegan and bought a cottage there on the corner of Pine Road and Forest Lane, to which they escaped whenever they could. It had a Bauhaus-style exterior of white stucco walls, steel casement windows, and flat roof, but inside it was filled with wide plank paneling of dark knotty pine—it was as if a progressive Berliner had married Heidi of the Swiss Alps and they decided to build a home together.

Saul and Stanley would have preferred staying with their parents in Mohegan, but during the summers of 1940 and 1941, Louis and Lilly sent the boys to Camp Mohaph in Glen Spey, New York, to learn Hebrew and become familiar with Jewish rituals. (The camp's name sounded Native American but was in fact just a combination of the owners' first names: Moe, Harry, and Phil.) Avid Zionists, my grandparents felt this was important for Saul and Stanley. Summer camp was also a way to avoid the significant threat of polio in those years before a vaccine became available in 1955. At Camp Mohaph, Saul and Stanley were unimpressed by the opportunity to play sports with the children of the wealthy families who owned and operated Revlon (cosmetics), Hartz Mountain (pet food), and Horowitz-Margareten (kosher prepared food). They wished they were home with their friends, where they could do whatever they wanted to do. They did have one cousin at camp, seventeen-year-old Steve Wagner (Aunt Ada and Uncle Jack's son), who'd landed a job at Mohaph as a waiter (a privilege for which his aunt Lilly and uncle Louis paid one hundred dollars—a fortune in those days). But Steve was no more content as "the help" than his cousins were as campers.

On Wednesday, June 4, 1941, just before the boys' second summer at Camp Mohaph, Saul turned thirteen. Handsome and confident, Saul had chanted his Torah portion in Hebrew beautifully at his bar mitzvah the previous Saturday at the West Side Institutional Synagogue. Louis and Lilly were filled with pride. My grandparents celebrated their first son's achieving Jewish manhood with what was proudly referred to as a "sit-down affair" at the St. Moritz hotel on Sunday, June 1. It was attended by the entire Zabar family, along with friends and all the employees in the store. Louis and Lilly had

Saul's bar mitzvah reception at the St. Moritz hotel, June 1, 1941.
Saul, Louis, Stanley, and Lilly are standing at the center of the dais,
in the upper-right-hand corner. (ZABAR FAMILY COLLECTION)

arrived, and they wanted to share their good fortune with everyone they held dear.

In the months leading up to Saul's bar mitzvah, between overseeing the popular King Stanley Self-Service Center and the bustling Zabar's, my grandfather was approaching his tipping point. Even a relentless workaholic like Louis could not be everywhere at once. He realized that it was time for him to take on a partner.

Louis turned to an old friend and onetime clerk at the Confidence Fruit and Vegetable Market in Brooklyn, a quiet, scholarly looking Russian Jewish immigrant named Yoshua Pevsner. Louis and Yoshua enjoyed conversing in Hebrew (studying Hebrew and Judaism was one of Louis's few extracurricular activities; he even found time to attend classes on these subjects) and their families were close. Louis so trusted Yoshua and his strong work ethic that years earlier, he'd asked Yoshua to be his partner in his Confidence produce business. Back then, Yoshua had lacked the money to buy in, but by the end of 1940, Yoshua had accumulated three thousand dollars in savings. He became Louis's partner at the King Stanley store on Columbus Avenue. In June 1941, they renamed it Zabar & Pevsner.

It was good timing for the joint venture. The elevated train tracks on Columbus Avenue that once made residents feel as if they lived under a dark, thunderous roller coaster had been demolished. In 1942, Yoshua and Louis opened another store, the King Kane Super Food Market, across the street at 313 Columbus Avenue.

It soon became evident that Zabar & Pevsner was more Pevsner than Zabar. The reserved, assiduous Yoshua carried most of the load while Louis tended to his other businesses. Esther, Yoshua's determined spouse, urged Yoshua to buy out his partner, but Louis wouldn't hear of it. He never sold a business, he said—he only bought them. But Yoshua persisted and, eventually, Louis reluctantly relented. Unfortunately, their friendship did not survive the breakup. Yoshua continued to run his own store until he died in 1990, at age ninety-three.

Louis's Upper West Side businesses had thrived and multiplied thanks to a roaring wartime economy, but World War II also created immense domestic challenges for people who made a living buying and selling food. The United States entered the war the day after December 7, 1941, and because the government now had to feed hundreds of thousands of men and women in uniform, supplies had to be regulated for civilians, and so a food-rationing system was put into effect. My grandparents had to walk the fine line between providing their demanding customers with the quality and quantity of food to which they had become accustomed, and fulfilling complex and constantly changing government regulations. Zabar's toughest times lay ahead.

Cheese Blintzes with Blueberry Sauce

Inspired by Lilly Zabar and adapted from Zabar's Deli Book *(1979)*
Edited and tested by Monita Buchwald

My father's story of blueberry blintzes triggers a fond sensory memory of the buttery aroma of sautéing blintzes wafting from my grandmother's kitchen in Mohegan Colony. Sometimes she served them with apricot jam sauce instead of blueberry sauce.

MAKES ABOUT 12 BLINTZES; SERVES 4

INGREDIENTS

For the batter
2 large eggs
1 cup water
¼ teaspoon kosher salt

1 cup all-purpose flour, sifted
2 tablespoons unsalted butter,
  melted

For the filling
8 ounces farmer cheese
1 large egg yolk

3 tablespoons sugar
½ teaspoon pure vanilla extract

For cooking
2 to 3 tablespoons unsalted
  butter, melted

For serving
Blueberry sauce (see following
  page)
Sour cream (optional)

DIRECTIONS

1. Make the batter: Beat the eggs and water together. Add the salt, flour, and melted butter, and mix well.

2. Heat a small (6- or 7-inch) skillet over medium-high heat. Brush the bottom of the pan with some of the melted butter. When the butter sizzles, add 2 to 3 tablespoons of the batter to the pan. Swirl it around until it lightly covers the whole pan.

3. Cook for 2 to 3 minutes, until the bottom is a light golden brown. Slide the blintz onto a plate. Repeat until all the batter is used. You should have 10 to 12 blintzes, depending on the size of your pan.

4. Make the filling: Mix together the farmer cheese, egg yolk, sugar, and vanilla. Put about a heaping tablespoon of the filling into the center of the uncooked side of the blintz wrapper. Roll up and tuck in the ends. Repeat with the rest of the wrappers and filling.

5. Finish the blintzes: Heat 2 tablespoons of the butter for cooking in a large skillet over medium heat. Place some of the blintzes in the pan, folded side down, and cook for 2 to 3 minutes, until golden brown. Flip the blintzes over and cook the second side until golden. Repeat with the remaining blintzes. Add more butter if needed.

6. Serve with the blueberry sauce and sour cream if desired.

Blueberry Sauce

MAKES 2 CUPS

1 pint blueberries (about 2 cups)
¼ cup water
3 tablespoons sugar
1 tablespoon cornstarch

1½ tablespoons fresh orange juice (or for a slightly tarter taste, use lemon juice)

DIRECTIONS

1. Place the blueberries, water, sugar, and cornstarch in a small pot. Bring to a gentle boil.

2. Reduce the heat and simmer until the blueberries start to break down but retain their shape, 3 to 5 minutes. Stir occasionally. Add the orange juice and stir.

3. Serve warm or at room temperature.

4

The War Years

WORLD WAR II TURNED THE ALREADY ARDUOUS LANDSCAPE OF NEW York City grocery stores into an even more challenging environment. The marketplace was competitive, the customers were demanding, supplies were limited, and the government's regulations and ration-coupon distribution system were complicated and erratic. Luckily, the time my grandfather spent as a youth working alongside his ambitious father in a similarly challenging economy had prepared him well.

Established in August 1941, the Office of Price Administration (OPA) was supposed to make sure goods were available to the widest range of people at affordable prices. By the spring of 1942, the government initiated a rationing system for consumers. But the proprietors were the ones who had to administer and enforce the OPA's rules and regulations. For example, Louis had to calculate his own ceiling prices based on what he'd charged for the same items before the price controls were instituted (which assumed he had kept precise records for that period and still carried exactly the same goods). For a new item, he was supposed to determine a price based on prices for similar products, or on prices charged by his competitors for the item. Plus, he had to keep abreast of the constantly fluctuating ceiling prices and an ever-changing list of regulated products. Louis was also responsible for collecting ration coupons from customers and turning them over to the government or to the wholesalers. He had to have enough ration points on hand to order replacement inventory from a wholesaler, know which color ration coupons were valid that week, and keep track of allowable prices. These requirements applied to many items in his stores, and he risked penalties if he failed to heed them.

Louis found ways to overcome some of these hurdles. For one thing, he realized that if he had his own wholesale business, he'd have better access to scarce supplies, especially fruits and vegetables, and could buy directly from manufacturers and producers. So, in 1941, my grandfather bought a partnership in the Sunshine Wholesale Cash Grocery Company and purchased their warehouse with his friend and former boss Abraham Zion. Located at 118 Hudson Street, the warehouse was one of the commercial loft buildings in what was then lower Manhattan's wholesale grocery district and is now the trendy Tribeca neighborhood. A Russian Jewish immigrant who had risen from peddler to a leader in the fruit and vegetable business, Abe Zion was a large, ruddy-faced fellow with an affable personality that was perfect for working the phones in the exhausting search for inventory. In addition to Abe's connections, Louis inherited from the former owner of Sunshine a contract with the major canned-goods manufacturer Del Monte. During the war, obtaining this kind of connection to a supplier of affordable goods was like striking gold.

As he had many times before, Louis turned a former boss or employee into a partner. Despite his independent, enterprising personality, my grandfather felt more comfortable when he shared the risks and rewards with a colleague. He favored this arrangement for the same reason that he preferred to hedge his bets by buying real estate as well as businesses: Like many immigrants who were legally unable to own land in Europe, Louis and Lilly felt safer when a building and the land it was on were truly theirs. Businesses could fail, but real estate would always be a source of income.

Louis would have liked to enlarge Zabar's long, narrow store at Eightieth Street and Broadway, but with limited space in the building, he decided to extend his reach elsewhere. In addition to his partnership with Yoshua Pevsner in two stores on Columbus Avenue, in 1942, my grandfather began to open grocery stores northward along Broadway. One was at 2551 Broadway between Ninety-Fifth and Ninety-Sixth Streets and the other was at 2844 Broadway between 110th and 111th Streets.

In 1945, Zabar's Super Market was in a single building in the middle of the block on the west side of Broadway between West Eightieth and Eighty-First Streets. Zabar's first location, in 1934, was in the Italianate building at the extreme right. Today, Zabar's occupies the five contiguous buildings extending northward from the corner of Eightieth Street and Broadway.
(OFFICE FOR METROPOLITAN HISTORY)

About the same time, Louis bought another small grocery store on the west side of Broadway, between Ninety-First and Ninety-Second Streets. The previous owner was Louis Chartoff, a friend and neighbor of Lilly's cousins Bertha and Abe Stillman. (His first name was pronounced "Louie," just as my grandfather's name was.) A mild-mannered and modest man, Chartoff was gruff, Louis Zabar's polar opposite, but my grandfather decided to retain him as a manager, thus maintaining customer loyalty and providing Chartoff with an income. For the rest of his career, Chartoff worked as a manager for the Zabar family in several stores. He would eventually play an even bigger role in all of our lives.

Louis sought out other ways to keep his enterprises flourishing. Coffee was so hard to come by during the war that physical
scuffles between shoppers over the scarce commodity were common in some stores. If his customers wanted their caffeine so desperately, my grandfather was determined to provide it. But doing
so involved taking some legal risks.

Louis's choices could have carried a heavy price because he was
not yet a citizen. As an illegal alien violating federal law, he could
have been deported. (According to Saul, Louis was already being
blackmailed for years by someone who was aware of his status. No
one in my family knows the identity of the blackmailer—perhaps it
was someone who knew him from Ostropolia, or during his short
stay in Canada—but they do know that Louis considered himself to
be in enough peril that he made regular cash payments to this person.) Although Congress had already created an amnesty program
for those who had arrived in America illegally before June 3, 1921,
my grandfather didn't qualify until Congress moved the cutoff date
for arrival to July 1, 1924. As soon as they did, Louis applied for
citizenship, on August 25, 1942.

A few months later, in November 1942, the OPA brought its very
first lawsuit in a Manhattan federal court. It was against my grandfather. Two wholesalers, Ostrover, Inc., and Elway Food Products,
were also named as defendants. Their offense was offering Belgian
Congo coffee for sale that was both rancid and priced above the
ceiling. Quality was so important to my grandfather that it's hard
for me to believe he knowingly sold rancid coffee; perhaps in everyone's haste to get the coffee to the customers, the shipment was
shelved before he had a chance to taste it. In any event, an account
of the entire affair was published for all to see in *The New York
Times, New York Post,* and even several out-of-town newspapers. The
Times reported the OPA's claim that "unless the defendants were
enjoined immediately, the public would be damaged, the war program impeded, and the price structure affected adversely." Federal
judge Simon H. Rifkind agreed, ruled that the defendants had broken the law, and signed an injunction designed to prevent further
violations of OPA regulations on coffee. It was meant as a warning

to other retailers and wholesalers who may have been similarly inclined to ignore OPA rules.

My grandfather was obviously not cowed by his first run-in with the OPA, because he soon disobeyed their regulations again by selling sliced packaged bacon above the ceiling prices. This time, as punishment, on May 24, 1943, the OPA ordered Louis to suspend the selling of any rationed foods for two weeks.

At fourteen and ten, Saul and Stanley were too busy attending school, playing stickball, and going to the movies to notice their father's name in the papers. But my anxious grandmother must have been distraught. She was expecting a third baby imminently (my uncle Eli was born on July 1, 1943), and here was her respectable husband repeatedly defying the OPA.

At least Louis was now a citizen. The U.S. District Court had finally granted his petition for naturalization on February 1, 1943, only a few months before the suspension. My grandfather's new legal status was crucial, and not only because of his OPA issues. In war-torn Poland or the Soviet Union, to which he would have been deported, Louis's relatives were being arrested and murdered by the Nazis. By the time Louis became a naturalized citizen, his uncle Avrum had been arrested in Ostropolia, along with 580 other Jews, by the German Einsatzgruppen. Avrum was in his early nineties and too weak to keep up on the twelve-mile forced march to Starokonstaninov. The Nazis shot him on the road. The rest of the Ostropolia Jews were brought to a ghetto with thousands of Jews from nearby towns, then transported to the Novgorodsky Forest, where they were shot and buried, dead or alive, in mass graves. Ultimately, the Nazis killed an estimated 1.6 million Ukrainian Jews. By the end of World War II, there were almost no Jews left in Ostropolia.

Fortunately, by that time Louis's younger brother, Archik, and his immediate family were no longer in Ukraine and survived the war elsewhere in the Soviet Union. (His mother, Malke, had passed away in about 1925.) In the 1970s and 1980s, the Soviet Union began to allow Jews to leave. Saul and my father sponsored the immigration to America of Archik; his wife; his son, Solomon; his daughter-in-law; and his grandson. They also sponsored Sam Zabarko, the grandson of Louis's stepbrother, Dudie, and Sam's wife and two daughters. ("Zabarko," which was more Ukrainian-sounding than the Jewish-sounding "Zabarka," was used by our Soviet cousins in an attempt to escape the mounting antisemitism in the Soviet Union.) Louis always had a job at Zabar's for a relative or friend in need of one, a tradition later continued by Saul and Stanley. They hired Sam Zabarko to work as a front-end manager at Zabar's, a position he held for almost thirty years.

In September 1944, my grandfather encountered one of his greatest challenges. The Upper West Side Consumers Council accused Louis, president of Zabar's Super Markets, Inc., of over-charging for groceries and failing to post ceiling prices in two of his stores, at 2245 Broadway and 2551 Broadway. Louis went before Magistrate Charles E. Ramsgate in New York City's Municipal Term Court, where a parade of ten housewives brandished cans of salmon and beans in the courtroom as evidence. (The government was encouraging consumers to report violations of the OPA regulations and to testify against transgressors.)

Louis's first attorney, Samuel L. Orlinger, was also a Russian Jewish immigrant. At five feet two and a half inches and 170 pounds, he was even shorter than my grandfather, and much wider. He planted himself before the magistrate like a fireplug and defended Louis by saying that the overcharges weren't Louis's fault at all. They were employee mistakes.

Magistrate Ramsgate didn't buy it. "Whenever I hear that plea," he responded sarcastically, "I always wonder whether they ever make errors in favor of the purchaser."

It was an ominous sign of things to come. Ultimately, my grandfather pleaded guilty to nineteen counts of failure to post ceiling prices and twenty-five instances of charging prices that were over the ceiling. He didn't do so out of remorse—in his opinion, the government's constantly changing regulations were onerous and unfair to independent grocers—but because it was clear the trial wasn't going his way. Louis and Orlinger expected to pay a fine and move on from what they believed to be yet another OPA farce.

They were wrong. Ramsgate sentenced Louis to the heaviest jail term and monetary fine ever imposed in a magistrate's court for violation of OPA regulations: twenty-eight days in jail and a fine of $1,055, the equivalent of $15,380 today. The judge did provide some leniency. He granted a four-day stay of the jail term to allow Louis to observe the Jewish high holidays.

Shocked and upset, Louis hired a new attorney to appeal the decision. This time, he chose someone who was the polar opposite of Samuel Orlinger. Tall, patrician Arthur J. W. Hilly was a well-known former city corporation counsel, a non-Jewish native New Yorker and graduate of Fordham University who definitely knew his own worth. As Saul tells it, "My mother said that every step Hilly took cost Louis five thousand dollars."

A few days after Louis's conviction, Hilly appealed the sentence and the fine, the OPA counsel opposed the motion, and Magistrate Ramsgate reserved decision until October 6, leaving my grandfather in the custody of his attorney. But the appeal was, ultimately, unsuccessful. My grandfather was headed to jail. Once again, the New York newspapers triumphantly announced the fate of "Louis Zabar, Price Violator."

For a businessman, a fine is a reprimand, but a jail term is a *shondeh*—an embarrassing scandal. Saul was sixteen when his father went to prison. He remembers Louis serving his term at what was then known as the Rikers Island Penitentiary, a jail for offenders with short sentences. Although my father was twelve at the time, he says that he has no memory of Louis's absence from home. Denial was most likely my father's way of coping with the trauma of Louis's conviction.

To avoid being cooped up inside, Louis asked to work on the grounds for his required labor. For eight hours a day, he tended the thousands of trees and shrubs on Rikers Island being cultivated for municipal parks and parkways. Working in the Rikers tree nursery wasn't too bad—for Louis, it was even familiar. It reminded him of his experience in his father's lumber business and his own stint as a lumberjack in Canada.

My grandfather was just one among many retailers and wholesalers who violated OPA regulations during the war, but his punishment stood out as far harsher than the typically mild reprimands other violators received. The OPA prosecuted one purveyor of ready-cut poultry for miscalculating the price for a packaged chicken with the neck, wings, thighs, and breast attached, but the complex chicken-pricing rules so bewildered even Magistrate Ramsgate that he declared, "The guy who got this up must have been the same chap who got up those income tax forms," and he dismissed the charge.

Louis, Magistrate Ramsgate, and the beleaguered poultry purveyor were hardly alone in their frustration with the OPA. Within a year of my grandfather's conviction, Abe Zion, who was the honorary president of the Associated Retail Fruit and Vegetable Merchants, led two thousand independent retailers in Brooklyn and Queens in closing their stores as a protest against the OPA's bewildering regulations. They maintained that the rules made it impossible for them to operate legitimate businesses without resorting to the black market to purchase goods. The retailers reopened only after the OPA agreed to take steps to remedy their grievances— unfortunately, too late to keep my grandfather out of jail.

BY THIS TIME, Saul had transferred out of Stuyvesant High School, the highly competitive specialized public school then located on East Twenty-Third Street in Manhattan. Stuyvesant was not a particularly good fit for Saul because, much to his parents' consternation, his schedule had left him free to spend his afternoons gallivanting around the city with his friends. A knowledgeable customer named Mr. Brown suggested that Saul attend Horace Mann, a private boys' school in the Riverdale section of the Bronx. It was at the time the school of choice for the sons of Jewish businessmen, professionals, and the occasional mobster. (Meyer Lansky's son Paul was a Horace Mann student in the 1940s.) Saul had begun his junior year there in 1944 and was delighted with the large campus nestled in fields of green. He soon became part of a close group of boys that included his best friend, Ira Levin, the future author of *Rosemary's Baby*. Saul's fellow students affectionately called him the Pickle King of Upper Broadway and Pickle-in-the-Middle Zabar.

Louis had acquired a nickname, too. He now had his hand in so many ventures—a partnership in two stores on Columbus Avenue, ownership of four stores on Broadway and a wholesale business, plus several projects that we no longer know much about—that Ada's husband, Jack, dubbed him The Octopus.

It wasn't intended as a compliment. Jack, an engineer, and Rose's husband, Irving Henner, an accountant, both worked for Louis. To their dismay, he was far more successful than they were, even though he did not have a professional degree. My grandfather had grown up as the darling of six sisters, and Ada and Rose still doted on him in New York. (Gittel, the eldest, had moved to Palestine, and Elka and Pessya, the two sisters who had survived the Ostropolia pogroms, remained in the Soviet Union.) Yet to his brothers-in-law, Louis was a gruff and uneducated peasant. He might have spoken five languages—Yiddish, Russian, Polish, Hebrew, and English— but his strong Yiddish accent came through in the other four. My demanding grandfather was equally unimpressed by his brothers-in-law, and no doubt felt their condescension. Even though Irving was Zabar's accountant, Louis continually referred to him as "the bookkeeper." Jack and Irving would have preferred working for engineering and accounting firms rather than for a grocer, but discrimination against Jews remained prevalent in those professions in the 1940s.

Only one of Louis's new ventures proved too painful for Lilly to tolerate—a bar and grill on the ground floor of a five-story building at 2708 Broadway, between 103rd and 104th Streets. Years earlier, when he was still an illegal alien, my grandfather had purchased the building and the bar in Ada's name. In 1945, two years after he had received amnesty and was able to own property legally, Louis transferred ownership of the building from Ada to a corporation owned by him; he listed himself as the proprietor of the bar and grill. Until the business was officially in his name, it's quite possible that my grandmother didn't know that her husband was the owner of a bar. This news did not go over well with Lilly. Still traumatized by her experiences with drunken Ukrainian peasants in her family's tavern, Lilly insisted that Louis sell the bar and grill, which he did, reluctantly. Loath to sell anything, he held onto the building as an investment.

As the war was winding down, Aaron Klein and my grandfather established a business called Overseas Parcels. People could use Overseas Parcels to send items such as butter, grain products, canned salmon, and evaporated milk to relatives in war-torn Europe. But some unscrupulous dealers overcharged purchasers and then included food worth less than what was promised. Twelve dealers were prosecuted by the OPA for this offense, including Zabar's Super Market, its manager Henry Cadoff, and two employees. Magistrate Ramsgate once again imposed a fine, this time three hundred dollars. My family's explanation was that someone else working at Overseas Parcels was responsible for the violations, and I believe this was true. For many years, Louis himself had been sending food packages to his needy relatives in the Soviet Union. He knew very well what receiving those packages meant to their recipients.

Louis also sent money to Palestine, for the education and support of his sister Gittel's family. But one evening in 1945, Saul discovered that Louis was also sending funds to other recipients in Palestine, and for a very different reason. By now a senior at Horace Mann, Saul had come home from school to find his father and several of his Russian Jewish friends engaged in a hushed conversation in their living room. Curious, Saul eavesdropped from the next room as Louis needled his friends to match his donation to what Saul assumed was a charitable cause. But Saul couldn't quite make out exactly which cause Louis wanted the men to support. When he heard Louis insist that if the Arabs "won," there would be no Jewish state and that the Jewish people would be running from one country to the next forever, Saul surmised that his father was secretly (and illegally) raising funds for the Haganah, the main paramilitary organization of the Jewish community in Mandatory Palestine, which was trying to drive the British out of the country and create an independent Jewish state.

My grandfather's ardent Zionism was a reaction to the discrimination and violence he and his family suffered in Russia. His clandestine support of a rebel organization that was battling an occupying power was typical of his defiance of laws he felt were unfair. Just as he had done in Ostropolia and in America during World War II, Louis continued to take action, legal or not, for causes and projects that he believed in, whether this was in support of his family, his fellow Jews, or his customers.

Lilly Zabar's Latkes (Potato Pancakes)

Edited and tested by Monita Buchwald

My grandparents did whatever they could to support the creation of a Jewish state in the land of Israel. For me, fighting for Jewish independence is associated with Hanukkah, the story of the Maccabees, and potato latkes. In the second century BCE, the Maccabees liberated the Second Temple in Jerusalem from the Syrian Greeks and rededicated it so that it could once again be used for Jewish services. To celebrate Hanukkah, Jews eat oil-fried latkes to commemorate the miracle of the Maccabees' stretching one day's worth of temple menorah oil to eight days. Grandma Lilly celebrated her birthday during the Hanukkah-Christmas season at the end of December. In Ostropolia, a child's birthday was observed not on the child's actual date of birth (which no one really remembered) but on the nearest Jewish holiday; for Grandma Lilly that was Hanukkah. Although her date of birth—and, therefore, her exact age—was a mystery, Grandma Lilly's crisp, hot latkes were definitely delicious.

MAKES 16 TO 18 LATKES; SERVES 4 TO 6

INGREDIENTS

2 yellow onions, cut into quarters
4 medium Idaho potatoes, peeled and cut into eighths
3 large eggs, beaten
1 tablespoon kosher salt

1 ½ teaspoons freshly ground black pepper
¼ to ½ cup all-purpose flour
Vegetable oil for frying
Applesauce or sour cream for serving

DIRECTIONS

1. Use a food processor, with the fine grater blade, to grate the onions, or grate by hand. Drain and discard the liquid. Transfer to a mixing bowl.

2. Grate the potatoes. Drain and discard the liquid. Add the potatoes to the onions and stir in the eggs, salt, and pepper.

3. Mix in ¼ cup of the flour to start. Continue to add more flour until the mixture has the consistency of thick oatmeal.

4. Heat about 1 inch of oil in a large skillet over medium-high heat. When the oil is very hot, drop in a scant ¼ cup of the mixture. Press down slightly to form an even latke. Cook on one side until a deep golden brown, 2 to 3 minutes. Flip it over and cook the other side. Remove from the pan and drain on a paper towel. Repeat with the remaining mixture.

5. Serve with applesauce or sour cream.

After the War

IN 1946, THE SAME YEAR THAT SAUL GRADUATED FROM HORACE MANN, my father, having completed Joan of Arc Junior High on the Upper West Side, entered Horace Mann as a freshman, where he joined many clubs and made the track team. Ever the protective mother, Lilly was convinced Stanley would die from track—so much huffing and puffing. Despite her fears, my father survived and earned his track letter. He was also a member of the photography club. He loved taking pictures with his big, square Speed Graphic camera, which came with a holder for a large blinding flashbulb, and his hobby often filled the basement in Mohegan with piles of negatives, photographic paper, and foul-smelling chemicals. My uncle Eli was one of his principal models and at one point starred in an affectionate series of photos taken in Riverside Park.

Saul had decided he wanted to get away from New York City. He planned to attend college in the Midwest and, later, medical school. It was a very competitive year for college applicants, and my uncle found himself vying for entry with the thousands of veterans whose education was being financed by the GI Bill. He ended up the only Jewish boy at Ottawa University, a small Baptist school built on farmland in the middle of Kansas. For two years, he studied hard and did well in his pharmacology major, but there were no Jewish girls to date, and he missed having a social life. So in 1948, for his junior year, Saul transferred to the University of Kansas, in Lawrence, which is about forty miles southwest of Kansas City. KU had a number of Jewish students and there was a good-size Jewish community in Lawrence. But as Saul's fraternizing and beer drinking increased, his grades went down. His waning interest in his

Lilly, Louis, and Eli, circa 1947.
(ZABAR FAMILY COLLECTION)

classes, as well as new developments at home, would soon draw Saul back to New York City. He never graduated.

I always found it fascinating that my New York Jewish uncle had spent his freshman and sophomore years at a Christian-based school in rural Kansas that had been founded by Baptist missionaries and built on land donated by converted Ottawa Native Americans. To me, it was as if he'd gone to college on the moon. Decades later, while visiting friends in Kansas City, my husband and I took a drive through miles of prairie to see where Saul had spent those two years. Ottawa is still a small town filled with low-rise Victorian-style commercial buildings grouped along a wide main street, with the university on the outskirts of town. There were only a few students wandering about on what appeared to us to be a chilly and spare campus. It hardly seemed like my outgoing uncle's kind of place.

Saul wasn't the only one trying out new locales. Louis had ventured into a new neighborhood, too. In 1946, he purchased a five-story building at 49 Nassau Street, in the financial district in lower Manhattan. On the ground floor he opened King & Co., a delicatessen managed by Aaron Klein, which stayed busy serving local office workers.

By now, my grandfather had created a sizable group of small delis and grocery stores, but he still couldn't compete with the burgeoning modern supermarket chains. And so, in 1948, Louis decided that the time had come for him to take his own plunge into the world of the supermarket. Back in 1942, when Louis had opened what he had grandly called Zabar's Super Market on the northeast corner of Broadway and 110th Street, the store was on the ground floor of what was known as a taxpayer, a one- or two-story building that was supposed to make the owner enough of a profit to pay the building's taxes and other expenses until the eco-

Louis (second from the left, looking up at the camera) *and store manager Aaron Klein* (center, with cigarette) *in King & Co., a delicatessen Louis opened at 49 Nassau Street in 1946.* (ZABAR FAMILY COLLECTION)

nomic situation became conducive to full-scale development of the property. Built in 1911, the Renaissance-inspired building boasted lovely polychromatic terra-cotta ornaments, a Spanish tiled roof, and an ornate lobby that led to the offices on the second floor. In 1948, the time was right to begin restructuring the store at 2844 Broadway into something that would truly pay off for Louis. This was going to be Zabar's first real supermarket and what Louis may have intended to be the first step in the creation of his own modern supermarket chain.

The individual vendors, pushcart peddlers, and public markets were largely gone by now, and the small neighborhood stores specializing in a single type of product—fruits and vegetables, fish, or meat—provided labor-intensive services to their customers that limited their profitability. Large, modern-looking, and efficiently run chains such as Gristedes and A&P were successfully challenging the ubiquitous local mom-and-pop grocery stores. As cities grew larger and transportation improved, the chains could take advantage of bulk buying and mass distribution to price their products competitively. The packaged food, dazzling array of attractively presented products, and self-service shopping were the hallmarks of these new supermarkets. Fewer employees were needed behind the counters, which meant supermarkets could offer lower prices that the independent retailers could not match. The small local shops didn't stand a chance.

Louis had for many years been observing the direction in which the grocery business was heading, which was why he'd dipped his toe into self-service with the King Stanley Self-Service Center back in 1939 and began calling some of his stores "Super Markets" in the early 1940s. Nevertheless, his shops were still relatively small, with traditional interiors. He was at a disadvantage to the chain stores, and he knew it. As early as 1942, the first year his grocery store at 110th Street was in operation, the newspaper *PM,* in an article about local food stores, had cited specific bargains to be had at Zabar's Super Market, especially in its large cheese department. But it also concluded by saying, "Not one of the places shopped matched big chain store prices."

Just as Louis was thinking about how to reconfigure his shops, disaster struck the store at 110th Street. At approximately 9:40 p.m. on January 26, 1948, a fire started in the basement of 2838-2844 Broadway. It spread quickly through the two-story brick building, engulfing a florist, a Loft candy store, a Whelan drugstore, and Zabar's Super Market. Traffic was halted at the corner of Broadway and 110th Street for several hours as a large crowd watched the four-alarm blaze wreak $200,000 worth of damage to the building and everything in it.

Four clerks and twenty customers were still inside Zabar's Super Market when the fire was discovered. Everyone quickly headed for the exits—except for one customer, who, according to *The New York Times,* insisted on purchasing a bottle of milk before she left. No one was harmed.

My grandfather was devastated by the loss of his Super Market, but the betrayal that followed was nearly as bad. The property at 2844 Broadway was owned by Solomon Petchers, a real estate investor and developer and a dear friend of Louis and Lilly's. The fire was hardly extinguished when Petchers canceled Louis's lease. A clause in their contract gave him the option of doing so in the event of a major casualty that caused substantial damage to the premises, and friendship hadn't stopped him. If Louis wanted a new lease on the space in order to rebuild, he'd have to pay the ridiculously high rent Petchers now demanded. Louis, who had always counted on the stability that came with doing business with partners and friends, was appalled. No friend would do such a thing, he insisted. He argued his case for weeks, but Petchers stood firm. With no other option available, Louis agreed to a new lease and the hike in rent. But the friendship was over.

There was, however, a silver lining to this tragedy. Louis had been looking for an opportunity to create a state-of-the-art food store from scratch. Now, in 1948, he was ready. He poured his energies into the renovation, and on November 9, 1948, he unveiled what he described in a full-page advertisement in the *New York Post* as the "most modern market." Zabar's Super Market was totally self-service, the "most beautiful, up-to-date, and complete super market the West Side has ever seen," with six food departments and a complete line of frozen foods. "Nobody, but nobody," Louis declared, "will have lower prices. In fact, our prices will be lower many times. Nobody, but nobody will have better quality. The policy of our store can be summed up briefly as, 'The highest quality at the lowest prices.'"

Louis and Lilly now had five grocery stores, a wholesale business, a downtown deli, and plenty of real estate. They had each other, and they had three healthy sons whom they adored (even if impetuous, energetic Saul and methodical, logical Stanley often butted heads). They had The Crowd, a social circle of affluent, self-made couples, many of whom had also been born and grown up in Russia. The Crowd moved as a pack from weddings to bar mitzvahs to summer colonies in Westchester and winter hotels in Miami Beach, playing gin and canasta in every locale. Lilly had achieved her dream of living in Manhattan, the boys were flourishing, and Louis remained as strong and energetic as ever, easily hefting wooden barrels of sour pickles or schmaltz herring. The future for the Zabars looked safe and secure.

Then one day toward the end of 1948, forty-seven-year-old Louis found himself struggling to lift a sack of coffee beans. His doctor, a kind and refined European named Leon Dinkin, performed tests that showed Louis's white blood cell count was high, but Dr. Dinkin couldn't determine why.

My grandfather's symptoms worsened. As he walked up Broadway to check on his stores, always puffing on an unfiltered Camel cigarette, he felt slow and uncoordinated. He tried to keep his balance but appeared so unsteady on his feet that kids on the street thought he was drunk and sometimes taunted him. He purchased the grill three doors up from Zabar's, at 2251 Broadway, and renamed it Zabar's Delicatessen, just to have a place where he could have a cup of coffee and relax during the day, whenever he needed to.

My grandmother was beside herself with worry. She blamed Solomon Petchers's disloyalty and Louis's subsequent stress as the catalyst for my grandfather's decline in health. Stymied, Dr. Dinkin suggested Louis consult with a specialist in Switzerland. On March 17, 1949, a cloudy and chilly day, Louis, Lilly, and twenty-year-old Saul, who had left the University of Kansas in his junior year to spend time with his ailing father, set sail on the *Queen Mary*. They left six-year-old Eli and seventeen-year-old Stanley behind, Eli gripping his brother's hand as they watched the enormous ship depart.

Eli was bereft. Instead of Mrs. Bloch, Eli's familiar but by now elderly nanny, my grandparents had asked a friend's sister to care for him. My uncle had never met the woman before. Stanley was now a senior at Horace Mann, and Lilly believed that he was mature and responsible enough to serve as a surrogate parent for Eli for three months. Eli tried to be the brave little boy his parents expected him to be. He moved into Stanley's bedroom, and Stanley made sure his brother was okay before he left for school each morning. Eli didn't understand how very sick his father was; all he knew was that he missed his parents and Saul terribly. Then Eli developed pneumonia. Stanley summoned Dr. Dinkin, who made several home visits to give Eli shots of penicillin, a miracle drug that had only recently become widely available for use as an antibiotic. When Stanley returned home each day from Horace Mann, he walked Eli over to Dr. Dinkin's Gothic-style office on West End Avenue for additional injections—until one day Eli refused to go. He was tired of being jabbed by needles. Despite Dr. Dinkin's objections, Stanley, the self-proclaimed diagnostician, concluded that Eli was fully recovered, as he appeared to be back to his former rambunctious self, and so he put an end to the injections. (This early success must have given Stanley a taste for problem-solving; to this day my father continues to monitor and attempt to resolve his kid brother's problems, as well as those of the rest of us—whether we have asked him to or not.)

While Stanley was overseeing Eli's medical treatment in New York, Louis, Lilly, and Saul had taken up temporary residence in Saint Moritz, where Louis consulted with the specialist at the clinic recommended by Dr. Dinkin, Saul occupied himself with skiing, and Lilly, whose sole sport was canasta, tried to find other things to do to occasionally take her mind off the anxiety she felt about Louis's condition. One day, she took the funicular up a mountainside to see the view from the top. As she gazed down on the gorgeous, snow-covered landscape, she heard a familiar female voice.

"Lilly Zabar, what are *you* doing here?"

It was Mrs. Ilse Winkler, a Zabar's customer, on a vacation with friends. Mrs. Winkler introduced Lilly to her companions as her grocer. Seeing a familiar face cheered my grandmother up a bit. Lilly and Ilse exchanged pleasantries on top of the mountain, just as if they were on Broadway on the Upper West Side.

That was not the last social interaction between the Zabars and the Winklers. Years later, Mrs. Winkler's daughter, Bea, who still lives in my parents' building, wanted to fix me up with her brother. She said he was a really nice guy and an actor in a very successful television sitcom. I was in graduate school at the time, and when it became clear I had never seen *Happy Days,* Bea realized I was probably not the right person for her brother, Henry. My children still joke about what it would have been like to have had The Fonz for a dad.

When the results of the tests that had been conducted on my grandfather came in, Louis, Lilly, and Saul gathered in the doctor's office, where they were informed that Louis was suffering from end-stage syphilis, and that his weakness and lack of coordination were the result of the disease having entered his cerebellum.

Louis, Lilly, and Saul were shocked—and also extremely doubtful about the accuracy of the diagnosis. My grandfather had always loved to flirt with the ladies, but any actual infidelity was out of the question. My grandparents adored each other, and Lilly knew for certain that her only rivals were the Zabar businesses. Louis, Lilly, and Saul dismissed the doctor's findings as ridiculous and left Switzerland to visit the newly established State of Israel. Despite the continued uncertainty surrounding Louis's failing health, this was a doubly thrilling trip for my grandfather. He got to see firsthand the Jewish state that had come into being just a year earlier, the homeland he had hoped and prayed for since he was a boy. And he was finally able to reunite with his oldest sister, Gittel. Gittel's husband, Betzalel Pasternak, had left the famine-ravaged Soviet Union illegally for Palestine in 1927, and Gittel and their children had followed him there legally in 1931. Louis had not seen his sister since 1921. And now he was also able to meet her children, Shlomo and Tzipora, for the first time. Saul became close to his cousin

Shlomo, whose tuition Louis had often paid and who was now a soldier in the Israeli army. Their time in Israel was a balm, although a brief one, for a family still wondering what was wrong with its patriarch. When they returned to New York in June, Louis insisted that Dr. Dinkin run more tests. This time, the results showed that my grandfather had lung cancer.

Louis didn't understand how this could have happened to him. At that time, doctors didn't know how people developed lung cancer. It was true that Louis was a four-pack-a-day cigarette smoker, but practically everyone he knew smoked. They didn't *all* have lung cancer. In 1949, the causal relationship between tobacco and lung cancer was virtually unknown. It wasn't until 1956, seven years after Louis's diagnosis, when 56 percent of the American adult population were regular smokers, that scientists established the epidemiological link between cigarettes and lung cancer. But none of that mattered for Louis in 1949. The only treatment available at the time was surgery, so he went to the Mayo Clinic in Rochester, Minnesota, where a famous surgeon opened him up and discovered that my grandfather's body was riddled with cancer. There was nothing to be done.

Back in New York, Louis tried to find some sort of treatment, however remote the odds for success. A former schoolmate of Saul's at Horace Mann was the son of Abram Nathaniel Spanel, the founder of the International Latex Corporation (later known as Playtex), who at the time was financing, among other medical experiments, cancer research. Spanel suggested Louis visit an Italian doctor in New York who had been importing from Italy medicine made from the glandular material of unborn sheep and that was administered by injection. The treatment was expensive and illegal and made Louis tired and irritable, but it did appear to arrest the progress of the disease for a few months.

In late fall of 1949, as the weather in New York started to turn crisp, my grandparents decided that spending a few months somewhere warm might help Louis feel better. They took Eli out of first grade at The Ramaz School (a Modern Orthodox Jewish day school in Manhattan) and went down to Miami together with Saul, who had decided not to return to college. Eli wasn't at all sorry to leave

Ramaz. He often got into trouble there because Lilly sent him to school with nonkosher sandwiches for lunch. (The Zabars were no longer keeping kosher at home.) Stanley had just started his freshman year at the Wharton School at the University of Pennsylvania and remained there.

Saul's friend Arthur King was in Miami, too. Seven years older than Saul, burly and with a beatnik-type beard, Arthur was an incredibly gifted, self-taught goldsmith from Greenwich Village who crafted elaborate, avant-garde silver and gold jewelry that often featured baroque pearls and uncut gemstones. He became quite famous in the 1960s and 1970s, eventually owning eighteen jewelry stores and selling his creations in high-end shops in Miami, Havana, and London, among other cities throughout the world, to customers including Elizabeth Taylor, Lena Horne, and Barbara Hutton. Lilly did not seem to appreciate this exuberant, artsy member of the counterculture hanging around while her husband was dying, but he appeared to divert my uncle's attention from the sad reality of Louis's failing health, and so Arthur was tolerated.

In Miami, Louis entered an experimental program of intravenous chemotherapy containing nitrogen mustard, the same deadly mustard gas that had been used as a weapon during World War I. Yale University scientists Louis Goodman and Alfred Gilman had proved it could fight cancer back in 1943, but wartime secrecy prevented them from revealing their experiments and publishing their results until 1946. The treatment held enormous promise, but it was still in the earliest stages of development for use with patients, and for Louis, it did not provide even a short respite from his illness. Instead, it made him feel so awful that he finally decided to stop treatment altogether. "I don't want to live this way," he said angrily. Shortly thereafter, Louis was admitted to a hospital in Miami. His body had filled with fluid, and he was desperately weak. As Lilly sat with him in his room, he turned to her and said, "Go home."

Lilly wanted to stay, but she knew her husband didn't want her to be in anguish as she watched him die. Even in his weakened state, my grandfather was forceful in his wishes. And so, as she had done throughout their twenty-three-year marriage, my grandmother did as her husband asked. She went back to her hotel, to be with Saul and Eli. A few hours after Lilly left, at 2:30 a.m. on Monday, March 27, 1950, at the age of forty-nine, Louis Zabar died.

My grandfather's obituary in *The New York Times* identified him as the owner of a chain of grocery stores, which would have made him very proud. Starting out on the lowest rung of the fruit and vegetable business in 1922, Louis had worked unceasingly to create a small grocery empire. Had he not died at such a young age, he might have left a chain of supermarkets such as Waldbaum's or The Food Emporium as his legacy.

Louis's funeral was held at the Riverside Memorial Chapel on West Seventy-Sixth Street and Amsterdam Avenue on Thursday, March 30. He was in an open casket, dressed in a suit. As Stanley looked into the casket, he realized that he had not seen his father since Louis had left New York for Miami in the fall. It was a hard way to say goodbye.

Louis's death was a major turning point for the Zabar family. Bound by obligation and love, they knew they had no choice but to move the businesses forward without my grandfather's brilliant instincts and leadership. They were now on their own.

Lilly Zabar's Sweet Noodle Kugel

Tested and edited by Monita Buchwald

After a Jewish person dies, the deceased's immediate family mourns their loss by sitting shiva, at home, for seven days. During this period, relatives and friends visit the family to offer their condolences and support. Often, they bring gifts of food for the mourners. Sweet noodle kugel is a delicious comfort dish appropriate for a shiva call. Kugel comes in many varieties (potato, sweet potato, carrot, spinach, and broccoli, and also in a savory pepper-and-salt noodle version); it can be served as a side dish, dessert, or snack.

   If you have time, soaking the cooked noodles in milk overnight will make the kugel creamier. If you prefer it less sweet, then reduce the brown sugar to ⅓ cup.

SERVES 6

INGREDIENTS

6 tablespoons unsalted butter, divided, plus more for the baking dish
½ pound medium egg noodles
Kosher salt
1 pound cottage cheese
½ cup packed dark or light brown sugar
3 large eggs

1 cup sour cream
1 teaspoon pure vanilla extract
1 cup canned pineapple, drained and cut into small cubes
⅓ cup raisins
¼ cup graham cracker crumbs
3 tablespoons sugar
1 teaspoon ground cinnamon

DIRECTIONS

1. Preheat the oven to 350°F.

2. Generously grease an 8- or 9-inch baking dish with butter and set aside.

3. Cook the noodles in a large pot of boiling salted water until tender, about 8 minutes. Drain and run under cold water. Drain again.

4. Melt 4 tablespoons of the butter. Mix together the cottage cheese, the melted butter, the brown sugar, eggs, sour cream, and vanilla and blend in a food processor or stand mixer. Pour into a bowl. Add the cooked noodles, pineapple, and raisins and stir to combine.

5. Pour the mixture into the prepared pan. Blend the crumbs, sugar, and cinnamon and sprinkle over the noodles. Dot with the remaining 2 tablespoons butter. Place on a baking sheet and bake for 1 hour, or until the top is lightly browned and crisp.

6. Remove from the oven and let stand for 10 minutes before serving.

Life After Louis

AT AGE TWENTY-ONE, SAUL WAS NOW THE MALE HEAD OF THE ZABAR family. Despite his deliberate avoidance of involvement in the family business until now, Saul was the son who had spent the most time with my grandfather; after Louis's death, he knew he had little choice but to accept the responsibility, alongside his mother, of managing the Zabar family's group of food stores.

Those first years following his father's death left Saul feeling overwhelmed; on a typical day he would dash from the store on West 80th Street to the one on 92nd Street to the one on 96th Street to the one on 110th Street and then back again. Saul had to learn on the job, a process he described as similar to diving into the deep end of a pool and then learning how to swim.

He eventually became very good in a role that had been thrust upon him, but I think he would have been happier as an engineer or a mechanic. His attention to detail would serve him well in his development of the smoked fish and coffee departments at Zabar's. But Saul also discovered that he had a talent for fixing things. Whenever he had the opportunity, one of his great joys was assisting the repairmen at the stores, instead of managing his employees or interacting with the customers. Years later, when a customer named Leslie Merims called the store in a panic to say a food processor she'd bought at Zabar's had jammed just a few hours before a dinner party, to her surprise none other than Saul Zabar himself quickly showed up at her apartment to fix the machine.

After Eli was born, and then when Louis became seriously ill, my grandmother had become more focused on taking care of her family and less involved in the daily running of the stores. Louis had

Bench sitters on the Broadway pedestrian mall in front of the Zabar's Super Market that was located between Ninety-Second and Ninety-Third Streets, sometime in the 1950s. (VINTAGE PHOTOGRAPH COLLECTION OF TRACEY AND DAVID ZABAR)

been Lilly's formidable anchor in the New World, and now that she was a widow at the age of forty-eight, she felt untethered without her husband. About a year after my grandfather died, Lilly decided she and Saul couldn't run the businesses alone. She asked Stanley to come home at the end of his sophomore year to help them.

My father had always embraced his role in the family business. At the age of twelve, he was opening the stores on Sundays all by himself so that Louis and Lilly could sleep in. To him, it made sense that Lilly would summon him home to help. He felt it was what a son was supposed to do and, unlike Saul, he enjoyed working in the store. He has always been a whiz at numbers and can remember Zabar's sales figures from years ago. In 1951, he transferred from the Wharton School to New York University so that he could attend college and work in the store at the same time. Even as an under-graduate, he felt ready to take on the Zabar family's enterprises and real estate portfolio.

The business wasn't the only reason Lilly needed the boys nearby. After Louis's death, Lilly became lonely. The Crowd and its invitations had disappeared. This group of couples wouldn't include someone without a spouse. One of Lilly's acquaintances was going through something similar. Louis Chartoff, the gentle grocer whom Louis had kept on as manager after buying his store, had recently been widowed. He had twin girls the same age as my father. Within several months of my grandfather's death, Lilly became engaged to Louis Chartoff.

Saul and Stanley were caught off guard. "What's the hurry?" they asked their mother.

"They won't invite me," she replied. My grandmother may have been a worrier, but she was a survivor, too. If she needed a husband to get back into the social swim, she'd have one.

After their wedding at the end of November 1950, the Chartoffs took Eli with them to Miami on their honeymoon. Lilly thought having a stepfather would be good for Eli. Only six years old when Louis died, he hardly knew his father as a healthy man. When they returned, Louis Chartoff joined Lilly and Eli in her new apartment at 118 Riverside Drive at Eighty-Fourth Street, a spacious two-bedroom rental. My grandmother just didn't have the psychic energy to raise two girls in their late teens, so Louis Chartoff's twin daughters, Evelyn and Carrie, students at Hunter College, remained in their Bronx apartment on their own, which seemed to suit them just fine. Lilly may not have embraced her new stepdaughters in some ways, but when the girls got married a few years later, Lilly threw lavish weddings for both of them.

Not only the speed with which she remarried but also my grand-mother's choice of husband surprised her children. Mr. Zabar, as she thereafter referred to her first husband, to distinguish him from her second one, had been assertive, ambitious, energetic, and temperamental. Louis Chartoff, on the other hand, was unas-suming, dapper, and quiet. Lilly enjoyed being in the driver's seat in her second marriage, but she also missed Mr. Zabar's manly pizzazz. And she had no problem letting Louis Chartoff know this. He seemed to take it all in stride. But whatever his shortcomings as a spouse, Lilly's new husband served his purpose: he was a well-dressed, affable escort, and Lilly was once again included in The Crowd's activities. Louis Chartoff's gentleness had another benefit to the Zabar family: in a few years, he'd become a loving Grandpa Louis to me, my siblings, and my cousins—the only grandfather we ever knew.

SHORTLY BEFORE LOUIS DIED, Saul had married Rosalie Rothstein, a sociable and stylish brunette whom he had met in Mohegan Colony. Now my uncle had to be the main breadwinner for two families. He needed Stanley more than ever, because in addition to the grocery stores, the Zabars still owned Sunshine Wholesale at 118 Hudson Street, as well as other real estate purchased by Louis over the years.

But while my father assisted Saul as much as he could, he now had an additional distraction. He had been dating a Hunter College student named Judith Segal for a year, and things had become serious between them. They'd met during Christmas vacation in Judy's freshman year, when she accompanied an NYU student to an Alpha Epsilon Pi fraternity dance at Bill Reiber's, a nightclub in Westchester. Judy wasn't interested in the NYU guy, but she had been looking for an opportunity to wear her new red tulle strapless formal dress a second time. And, besides, as her mother always said, "You don't meet anyone staying home."

At the nightclub, Judy was seated opposite a nice-looking young man with an olive complexion and dark hair. He smiled at her with a slightly lopsided grin that revealed teeth as white as his dinner jacket. He was with a quiet blond date, but Judy flirted with him anyway, by playing every party game she knew. It turned out the smiling man was named Stanley Zabar, and he was home for the holidays from the Wharton School while his mother, stepfather, and little brother were vacationing in Miami.

After taking his date home, Stanley offered to drive Judy and her date home in his cream-colored Chevy convertible. And after they dropped Judy off, Stanley made sure to confirm with his fraternity brother that there was nothing serious between him and the pretty Hunter undergrad. And so began my father's courtship of the woman who would eventually become my mother.

Stanley sent Judy an invitation to their first date on gold-encrusted AEPi fraternity stationery, which she found quite impressive. He took her to a concert at Carnegie Hall and then to a nightclub that featured two figure skaters performing in the center of the floor. On their second date, he drove her to the house in Mohegan, stopping on the way at Zabar's 110th Street Super Market for a precut, prewrapped sirloin steak, a package of frozen peas, and a can of peaches. That proved to be even more impressive. Judy had never been to a real supermarket before. In the Segal household on the Upper East Side, a kosher butcher delivered meat wrapped in brown paper. She had never seen frozen vegetables.

In the spring of 1952, after a yearlong courtship during which Stanley switched from Wharton to NYU, he came down with mononucleosis. When Judy visited him in the Riverside Drive apartment, he was sprawled on the sofa, exhausted. She was standing on the other side of the living room, guarding against contagion, when my father proposed marriage. He was tired of commuting crosstown to see her, he said. Then he presented Judy with Lilly's diamond solitaire ring, which she had stopped wearing when she married Louis Chartoff. Actually, he tossed it across the room to her so that she could remain at a safe distance. (About a decade ago, my mother gave me this diamond ring. I wear the round glittering stone on the High Holy Days to bring an emblem of my grandmother's presence into the synagogue.) Despite my father's decidedly unromantic proposal, my mother accepted. They both wanted to get married so that they could live in the same place.

When Stanley and Judy announced their betrothal to my mother's parents, my Grandma Selma vetted my father the only way she knew how. She checked the Yellow Pages.

"They own a store," she said. "They must be all right."

Judy was nineteen and Stanley was twenty. My mother was an only child living with her parents in a small apartment at 166 East Ninety-Second Street, around the corner from the 92nd Street Y.

Born and raised on the Lower East Side, Louis and Selma Jacobs Segal had made it through the Great Depression and World War II, and owned a candy and newsagent store nearby on Lexington Avenue. Louis, a bald, stocky man, had suffered a heart attack several years earlier and was not supposed to get into stressful situations. My mother's engagement at such a young age was a shock to her parents. Upon hearing their plans, sixty-three-year-old Louis referred to his future son-in-law as "a little *pisher*"—Yiddish slang for a young boy with little life experience. Within her family, my mother was the first member of her generation to go to college, and her parents had thought that after she graduated, she would go on to a job in her chosen profession rather than marry early. Grandpa Segal died of a heart attack a year after the wedding.

Because my father was under twenty-one, Lilly had to go with him to sign the marriage license. After their wedding, on June 22, 1952, at the Hotel Esplanade on West End Avenue, my parents rented a one-bedroom apartment at 310 West 106th Street, between Broadway and Riverside Drive, and furnished it in the prevailing Danish modern style, just like Saul and Rosalie had done theirs.

My parents had planned for a leisurely honeymoon on Martha's Vineyard, but my father insisted they return to New York City early, in time for the opening of a new Zabar's supermarket at Ninety-Sixth Street and Broadway. With Lilly's encouragement, Saul and Stanley continued Louis's manifest destiny philosophy of supermarket development on the Upper West Side. The new store was called SELS Super Market—for Saul, Eli, Lillian, and Stanley. Louis's associate Aaron Klein, who had moved to Texas after my grandfather's death, returned to New York to help Saul and Stanley renovate the store that had been on the property into a modern supermarket. Once it opened in the summer of 1952, Aaron's cousin and protégé, Murray Klein, became the store manager. Little did Saul and Stanley know what a major role Murray Klein would play in Zabar's many years down the road.

At meals with her new in-laws, my mother would try to decipher what seemed to be a peculiar Zabar family code. "How is One Eighteen?" Lilly would ask Saul and Stanley. "What's happening with

Forty-Nine?" Lilly was checking up on the various stores and real estate that Louis had left her, referring to the properties by their addresses. My grandmother also insisted Saul and Stanley have weekly meetings with their business partners in all their locations. She didn't trust anyone who wasn't family.

Lilly was like no one in Judy's family. "She actually asked her sons for advice," my mother recalled. "She rarely planned ahead, was often hazy about details, was always ready for a good time, and could put on her hat and dash out the door in an instant." Lilly was at her cheerful best when welcoming unexpected guests, always prepared at the ring of a doorbell to pull something delicious out of her refrigerator for an impromptu feast. Food was love, and to visit Lilly without taking the time to eat a meal was the worst possible affront. "My folks are happy if we just pop in and out to say hello," Judy would tell her mother-in-law, in the snippy tone that only a very young daughter-in-law could get away with.

Compared with my mother's modest, frugal, and emotionally reserved household of first-generation German Jewish immigrants who strove to become as "American" as possible, the Zabars were exotic, extravagant, and ambitious. They said whatever came into their heads with only the bare minimum of occasional decorum or tact. Rather than carefully tending to the demands of a single candy store, as my Segal grandparents did, the Zabars enthusiastically built a chain of stores.

Still, as the daughter of parents who worked in their store six days a week, my mother was familiar with the demands of retail shopkeeping. When she was young, if the boy who usually delivered the early morning newspapers to her father's customers was ill, my mother was drafted into service and would arrive at school late, with a note from her father. As a newlywed, she certainly understood when my father asked her to accompany him during the times that he occasionally had to fill in for the Zabar's deliveryman.

One night during a midsummer heat wave, they took Stanley's convertible (which he'd earned for two summers of work in The Store, which was how the family referred to the Eightieth Street location) to deliver an order to a Park Avenue address. A blast of air-conditioning greeted them as the woman of the house opened the door. When she invited them in to cool off, Judy had a flashback to her own youthful experience delivering newspapers to Park Avenue matrons in beautifully furnished and decorated apartments. To save money, the Segals' landlord had painted their apartment in a strange palette of indefinable colors—the result of the housepainter's combining the contents of whatever cans of paint he had left over from previous jobs. Judy never forgot the walls on those Park Avenue apartments, painted in the deepest, richest earth colors and jewel tones. She painted my parents' first bedroom a velvety chocolate brown that came out of its very own can.

After their wedding, my mother continued her undergraduate studies at Hunter College during the day and looked forward to my father's return in the evening. But by now, Stanley was a senior at NYU and was also running all of the Zabar's businesses together with Saul. On his way home each evening, after his classes and his work at the Zabar's store on Eightieth Street, he would stop at each of the other three stores along Broadway, to prove that he was on top of things and able to supervise store managers who were more than twenty years his senior. By the time he arrived at his and Judy's apartment, hours after he'd promised, dinner was cold and my mother was in tears.

It was around that time that Louis Chartoff became the manager of the rebuilt Zabar's Super Market at 110th Street and Broadway. Things were going along well until an incident in 1953 that involved Louis and his next-door neighbor at 2848-2850 Broadway, a former prizefighter named Al Turco, who ran a fruit and vegetable business called the Orange Grove, part of the Orange Grove chain owned by the Sloans. According to the account that appeared in *The New York Times* in March of that year, Louis noticed that Al had added canned goods to his stock. The way Al told it, Louis entered his store and told Al that he couldn't do that. If he did, Louis would make trouble for him. (Although this does not sound like the Louis Chartoff I knew, and he denied to the press that he had said that, I remember that he could be stubborn when crossed.) Al stood his ground, so at 1:00 p.m. that same day, Louis lowered the price of Zabar's fresh strawberries from twenty-five cents a pint to nineteen cents, which was below cost. Al responded by reducing his price to fifteen cents. When Louis met *that* price, Al—standing on a box and shouting to attract customers—began giving his strawberries away free, one pint per person. Over the next several hours, the same price war was repeated with tomatoes, figs, bananas, grapefruit, and cucumbers. Housewives from the nearby apartment houses jammed the block, carrying two to three shopping bags each, pressing their children into service, running back and forth between the two stores to snatch up whatever was free or cheapest. When the police arrived to find out what all the commotion was about, Al yelled, "Whadaya want? Is it against the law to give something away?" It wasn't, so the police just stood there and watched, along with everyone else. At 3:30 p.m., after each store had lost about one hundred dollars in the battle, the war ceased, just as swiftly as it had begun, and everything went back to normal. But sometime after the melee, the building's landlord called Al to say that his lease restricted him to selling only fresh fruits and vegetables, and not canned goods or groceries. Al promptly went into Zabar's. "Will you buy my canned goods for what I paid for them?" he asked Louis. "Sure," Louis responded. "Tomorrow morning."

About a decade later, another devastating fire swept through Zabar's Super Market on 110th Street. This one started as a grease fire in a restaurant in the same building. After this fire, Saul did not want to rebuild. He ended up transferring the supermarket lease to Al Turco. It took a while, but Al had finally triumphed over Zabar's—he could now legally sell in his store all the canned fruits and vegetables he wanted to sell, as well as his fresh produce.

A bit less than a year after the price war between Louis Chartoff and Al Turco, in January 1954, my mother graduated Phi Beta Kappa from Hunter College with a major in English, a minor in art, and me in utero. Six months later, on July 16, she awoke at 2:00 a.m., roused my father, and told him it was time to go to the hospital. This was a momentous occasion, my father said, and he wasn't going anywhere until he'd showered and shaved. My mother waited patiently, counting the minutes between her contractions until my father finished his ablutions, put on a white shirt, suit, and tie, and escorted her to their car.

I was born a few hours later in Columbia-Presbyterian Medical Center on 168th Street between Broadway and Riverside Drive. At the time, natural childbirth was considered somewhat avant-garde, but my mother had learned breathing exercises to control the labor pains from a class she and my father had taken (which also earned my father a certificate admitting him into the delivery room, another rarity in those days). She performed so outstandingly that her doctor asked her if she would describe her experience to the obstetrics nursing class. Sitting in a wheelchair, she was delighted to do so.

I was, alas, a colicky baby, and after three tension-filled days at home, during which I cried constantly from early evening until midnight, my parents hired a baby nurse for two weeks. This gave them a brief respite, but when the nurse left, I was still screaming my lungs out. The only way my parents could get me to sleep was to take me for a stroll in my Silver Cross carriage or a ride in their convertible.

The colic eventually went away, and my mother soon became bored with sitting on a bench in Riverside Park alongside a baby carriage. What she longed for was a house with a backyard where children could play without having to go to a park. And so when I was a year old we moved to a small attached Tudor-style rental house in Forest Hills, Queens. At that time, my father was studying law at Brooklyn Law School and also working at Zabar's. One of the things my mother liked best about our new neighborhood was that it was one hour and three subway lines away from the Zabar's stores. When my father was finished for the day at the Eightieth Street store, he came straight home.

After my inauspicious beginning, I had become so adorable that my parents decided to have a second child. (At least this is how they explained it to me at the time.) My brother, David Gershon, was born on Friday, January 13, 1956. (While we were growing up, I often pointed out to David that *his* cuteness did not inspire our parents to have our sister, Sandy, until nine more years had passed.) Soon after David's birth, my father graduated from Brooklyn Law School. He had gone to law school to enhance his role as the partner in charge of business operations at Zabar's, and he wasn't looking for a job as an attorney. But Zabar's lawyer, Harry Wachtel, surprised him with an offer to practice at his midtown firm of Wachtel and Michaelson. My father greatly admired Harry and was thrilled with the opportunity. The other associates at the firm had attended prestigious law schools, such as Harvard and Columbia. (My father could have gone to Columbia but, unlike Brooklyn Law School, Columbia frowned upon students who worked and was unwilling to permit him to arrange his class schedule to accommodate his part-time job at the store.) At the time, it made sense for my father to leave Zabar's. The business wasn't profitable enough to support my grandmother, Saul, and my father, and the new job provided him with his first chance to work outside his family business and in a specialty that he loved. And so Stanley left the running of the stores mainly to Saul, with the assistance of Murray Klein. We continued to see Lilly and Louis, Saul and Rosalie, and Eli on holidays, on visits to the Upper West Side, and in Mohegan Colony. Zabar's was still a part of my father's life, but his focus was now on his legal career and his young family.

Meanwhile, Saul had discovered that the same exacting, methodical nature that made him so good with mechanical devices also helped him evaluate Zabar's other products with just as much care. He became as passionate about quality as his father had been, and he came to love the process of inspecting and sampling fish from the smokehouses. Zabar's continued to offer several types of salmon: salty, flavorful lox; the subtler Nova Scotia; delicate Scottish smoked salmon; kippered salmon; pickled salmon; and salmon roe, known as salmon caviar. The store also sold smoked herring with roe, smoked eel, smoked kippers from Britain, and their own pickled herring. In the spring, smoked sturgeon and the small smoked whitefish known as chubs were at their best. Back then, Zabar's also sold a good amount of kapchonka, a large whitefish that was brined in salt and then hung from a hook and air-dried to draw out all the moisture and fat. People of Russian ancestry loved to chew on it like beef jerky.

Just as his father used to do, once a week Saul went to the smokehouses in Brooklyn and Queens to inspect and sample the domestic smoked fish destined for Zabar's—sturgeon, whitefish, sable, salmon, herring, and brook and rainbow trout. (By the early 2000s, only one major wholesale smokehouse, Acme, was left on the East Coast, and only my uncle, among hundreds of Acme customers, was given permission to wander about the premises, to taste, select, or reject the smoked fish for his store.) Wearing a white apron and a hairnet, Saul would push a rolling cart into the walk-in refrigerator where dozens of just-smoked sturgeons hung; it was the most expensive smoked fish sold by Zabar's. (Because it lacks scales, sturgeon is not kosher and must be kept separately from the other fish at the smokehouse, to accommodate the kosher retailers.) Inside the refrigerator he would unhook a succession of sturgeons and place each on a steel table, pressing and massaging the fish to see how it felt. Finally, he would carve out a small sample with the pointy end of an open paper clip, pop it into his mouth, and then spit the sample into a bucket after a moment or two of careful consideration. Sometimes the fish was too dry, and other times it was too mushy or soggy. There were days when Saul rejected the entire batch of a particular smoked fish and then came back the next day to taste a new batch. If he didn't like the sample, he rehung the fish on the rack. But if a sample met his standards, he would leave whatever quantity he was interested in on the table to be packaged and delivered to Zabar's the same day.

Texture was also a crucial factor for smoked salmon, which should be smooth, moist, and tender when sliced—never mushy. The grain should be evident in each slice, and the flesh should not reveal separations or gaps. The evaluation process was taxing, but it appealed to Saul's perfectionist nature. People came to Zabar's for its top-quality cured and smoked fish, and Saul knew that he'd better maintain his father's standards if he was to keep the business alive. Saul sometimes rejected 50 percent of the smoked fish delivered to Zabar's, even after it was smoked to his specifications. It was returned to the smokehouse for sale to less difficult customers.

Throughout the 1950s, Zabar's was still an appetizing store and delicatessen augmented with basic groceries and canned goods. Its clientele was mostly Jewish, as were the employees, who peppered their conversations with Yiddish expressions. A complaining customer was a *kvetch,* justified bragging was *kvelling,* and someone who did something stupid had no *seykhel.*

Few employees exemplified Zabar's as it was from the 1950s through the 1990s like Sam Cohen, a Holocaust survivor of slight build, great charm, and considerable intelligence, who was hired in 1953. Clad in a white coat, he would take his place behind the appetizing counter, where he masterfully sliced lox and smoked salmon sixty hours a week for forty-six years. Zabar's was Sam's stage and the customers were his audience. He flirted with the women and kibitzed with the men in Russian, Polish, Hebrew, Spanish, and English. When I was deemed old enough to order at the counter on my own (all the Zabar children had to wait on line along with everyone else, because Zabar's made no profit on our discounted purchases and we certainly weren't going to be allowed to jump ahead of real customers, who were paying full price), I would stand quietly, my numbered slip of paper clutched in my hand, until my turn came. Then there would be the moment when Sam would make eye contact with me, smile and nod, and reach across the counter for my number—sometimes even when I wasn't next. "My Lori!" he would exclaim. "My favorite customer, how is your education going? In what year of school are you now? Let me give you a taste of the North Atlantic novie—it is the best right now. It is what you will like." Sam made me feel special and appreciated.

Sam sometimes employed classic appetizing humor in his banter. Many years ago, a customer named Madelynn Heintz lost her job and would come to the Upper West Side to collect her unemployment insurance, an experience that depressed her every time. One day, to cheer herself up, she stopped at Zabar's and took a ticket at the appetizing counter, thinking how wonderful it would be to have a little bit of lox. When her turn came, she asked Sam for an eighth of a pound. He looked down at her, dead serious, and replied, as have generations of appetizing countermen before him, "You mean half of a quarter, lady? Are you having a party?" Despite her penurious state, Madelynn found Sam's wry humor amusing. And she was indeed cheered up.

Sam was the best-known appetizing man at Zabar's, and his fame spread far beyond the store. In his 1971 *New York Times* cartoon "Counter Culture: The Upper West Side Intelligentsia Meet at Zabar's," Al Hirschfeld included a smiling Sam standing behind the counter, waiting on celebrity customers that included Eli Wallach, Anne Jackson, Joseph Heller, Alfred Kazin, and James Wechsler. When he died in 1999, Sam received an affectionate obituary in *The New York Times*.

In addition to their myriad responsibilities, Saul and Stanley kept a paternal eye on their brother, Eli. Only eleven years older than I, he always seemed to be too young to be my uncle. Eli was blue-eyed and fair-haired, but he was far from angelic. My grandmother would say that Eli had *shpilkes,* a Yiddish word that roughly translates to "ants in his pants." From a young age, he channeled his energy into entrepreneurial endeavors and, like his father and grandfather, sometimes Eli went beyond the Pale—including at his own bar mitzvah.

That celebration took place on a warm July day in 1956. The grounds of Grandma Lilly's house in Mohegan Colony were filled with friends and family helping themselves to smoked fish and roasted chicken when the local police arrived. My father, then a law student, managed to intercept them before anyone else noticed. They were, one officer informed Stanley, investigating the alleged sale of illegal fireworks by Eli Zabar. Was he available for questioning? Of course not, my father explained, this gathering was actually his bar mitzvah party. He couldn't possibly have been selling firecrackers while he was the center of attention. Besides, my father said, he'd been with Eli the entire time and hadn't seen any fireworks being sold. My father was persuasive enough that the police left, but what he hadn't mentioned was that all afternoon, boys Eli's age had been coming by on their bicycles, entering the garage with the guest of honor, and then leaving a few minutes later. It is doubtful that the boys were dropping off bar mitzvah gifts. Lilly and her guests continued to party, unaware that Eli had barely escaped arrest as a juvenile delinquent.

My father took his job as paternal surrogate seriously, and he tried to be present for Eli as often as he could. And so one crisp fall day, we stood with Lilly on the sidelines of the Fieldston football field to watch Eli play for the private day school in Riverdale that had a decidedly liberal bent and substantial Jewish student body. Despite being five foot seven and of medium build, Eli had already won several games for the team and was now a football hero. His nickname was Meat.

Grandma Lilly was dressed for the occasion in plaid brown-and-tan slacks and a beige car coat, colors that went nicely with her fluffy white hair. She would complain about her aching feet whenever she wasn't being chauffeured, but this time she didn't say anything as we stood on the sidelines and watched Eli play. Even after my father tried to explain the rules several times, David and I didn't understand the game, and I suspect that my grandmother didn't, either, although she kept her eyes fixed on Eli wherever he was. Lilly was always concerned about the physical well-being of her sons, especially when they exerted themselves in demanding sports.

The novelty of this outing was beginning to wear off when suddenly the crowd began to roar. Eli was running across the field with the football cradled in his hands as the Fieldston cheerleaders and fans chanted "Zabar, Zabar, be our savior!" As I turned to watch Eli race toward the goalpost, I noticed that my grandmother was no longer by my side. She was hurtling along the edge of the field in her orthopedic cream-colored leather oxfords, right alongside Eli. "Stanley, look at your mother!" I heard my mother yell above the crowd. "She's making the touchdown with Eli!"

Eli graduated from Fieldston in 1961, still a popular football hero. As he made plans for college and his future, he had no idea of the outsized role he would later play in a culinary revolution already brewing in New York.

Zabar's Nova Cream Cheese Spread

Created by Tiffany Ludwig
Edited and tested by Monita Buchwald

Nova salmon is Zabar's quintessential product and has been so since 1934. If I had to choose my favorite offering in the store, it would be the hand-sliced Nova Scotia. But high-quality novie is expensive, so the usual rule of thumb of one-quarter pound per person can make for a very pricey brunch. Tiffany Ludwig, Zabar's artistic director, has created a sophisticated, easy-to-make spread that stretches a quarter pound of Nova Scotia much further and is delicious with brunch, cocktails, or lunch. This recipe can be made the day before and refrigerated.

MAKES 2 CUPS; SERVES 4 AS A MAIN COURSE,
6 TO 8 AS AN HORS D'OEUVRE

INGREDIENTS

*8 ounces Zabar's cream cheese
    (at room temperature for easier
    mixing)*
4 ounces sour cream
1½ teaspoons fresh lemon juice
*1 to 2 tablespoons capers,
    drained and rinsed*

2 tablespoons minced red onion
1 tablespoon chopped fresh dill
*4 ounces Zabar's smoked nova
    salmon, finely chopped*
*Bagel chips, bagels, rye bread,
    crackers, or carrot sticks for
    serving*

DIRECTIONS

1. Mix together the cream cheese and sour cream in a medium bowl until smooth.

2. Add the lemon juice, capers, red onion, and dill. Stir until combined.

3. Gently fold in the nova salmon until evenly mixed.

4. Serve on bagel chips, bagels, rye bread, crackers, or carrot sticks.

7

The 1960s Culinary Revolution and Zabar's Evolution

FIRST, I'D SLIT THE GLISTENING BROWN SKIN OF THE SMALL SMOKED whitefish with the side of my fork. Then, using the tines, I would fold back the skin to reveal the white flesh divided by a thin vertical brown stripe running parallel to the spine. The meat from the belly of the fish to the stripe is pleasingly soft and plump, salty yet sweet; the flesh closer to the spine is thin and hard to scrape from the underlying bones. After I ate both sides (careful not to swallow any of those thin white bones that are so hard to see), I would lift up the skeleton to reveal the bottom half of the fish and eat the rest. At age four, I was so proficient at eating a whitefish, my parents joked that they would put me in the window of Zabar's to show people how it was done. This was my weekly ritual at our family's Sunday brunches, when we often ate appetizing from the store: smoked whitefish, Nova Scotia salmon, smoked sturgeon, pickled salmon with onions in a clear brine, and bagels with cream cheese.

Aside from our Sunday brunches, which would probably have seemed rather exotic to people in the American heartland in the early 1960s, for the first few years of my life the food my family ate at home and when we dined out at restaurants was pretty standard American fare for that time. My mother had a rotating repertoire of family dinners: chicken or fish (generally, flounder or sole) baked under a layer of Campbell's cream of mushroom soup; spaghetti and meatballs smothered in Del Monte's canned tomato sauce; lamb shank stew; sirloin steak or hamburgers; and baked or fried salmon croquettes made from canned salmon. Most of the vegetables she served came from cans or the supermarket freezer case. All our desserts originated in cans, or as powders that came in boxes. For my father, it was always canned fruit, or Jell-O, or canned fruit *in* Jell-O. David and I preferred (and had fun making) MY-T-Fine chocolate or vanilla pudding, tapioca, or junket (a wobbly, milky, pastel-colored pudding that was uniquely able to stand on its own after we dislodged it from its glass cup).

Dining out was an infrequent but casual affair, mainly to neighborhood Italian or seafood restaurants. Once in a while, we ventured into Manhattan for Chinese at Tien Tsin on West 125th Street or Lucky's in Chinatown. Occasionally, on a weekend, my father took me to his childhood haunt, Steinberg's Dairy Restaurant, across the street from Zabar's, where elderly Jewish waiters with napkins on their arms shuffled back and forth, taking orders for beet borscht, scrambled eggs with lox, or blueberry blintzes. Steinberg's was a favorite of the actor Walter Matthau, who prided himself on being the only man who spoke French to the Jewish waiters: "Garçon, some chopped eggplant, *s'il vous plaît*."

Sometimes my family enjoyed shrimp scampi and South African broiled lobster tail at Sea Fare, at First Avenue and Fifty-Seventh Street in Manhattan. I remember how elegant I thought it was, with its white walls, white tablecloths, and waiters in white jackets. Sea Fare and its sibling restaurant, Sea-Fare of the Aegean, on West Fifty-Sixth Street, were frequented by celebrities such as Ava Gardner, Frank Sinatra, and Raquel Welch. One time, a waiter whispered to us that Walt Disney was a few tables away. My brother was too shy to go over by himself to ask for an autograph, so I agreed to accompany him. Mr. Disney graciously obliged, signing a menu for us in his famously elegant signature.

Most of my parents' entertaining was done at home, and my favorite events were their cocktail parties. Even as a small child I tried to participate. When we were still in nursery school, my mother once heard me pretend to call David on the telephone. "The kids are with my mother," I announced. "Would you like to come over for cocktails?" I loved to help my mother prepare for a cocktail party. I had no interest in setting out the drinks, but I was a crack assistant with the hors d'oeuvres: homemade deviled eggs sprinkled with paprika, big black olives from a can, and my favorite, smoked oysters. My job was to dislodge the metal key that was attached to the bottom of the oval oyster tin, insert the metal tab at the edge of the lid into the narrow slot that had been cut into the side of the key, and carefully turn the key, which rolled the lid open to reveal the shiny, dark brown, wrinkly oysters in clear brown liquid. As my reward, I was allowed to eat a few of those slippery, intoxicating mollusks. One time, I couldn't stop myself and devoured a whole tin before a party. I do not recommend this.

The women would arrive in tight-fitting cocktail dresses and pointy-toed pumps, sporting bouffant hairdos; the men wore blazers or plaid sport jackets, casual slacks, and narrow ties. They drank martinis and Scotch in our living room, with its Danish modern furniture and ivory slubbed linen drapes on which a pattern of colorful swimming fish had been hand printed. David and I, already in pajamas, liked to creep down the staircase and peek through the stair railings, trying to listen in on the adult conversation. We thought there was nothing more glamorous.

When my mother wasn't entertaining, she was dieting. No one would have called her overweight, but she had a vision of ideal slimness that she intermittently achieved. Every few months, she started a new diet: the grapefruit diet, Weight Watchers, and Metrecal. Metrecal made canned drinks in various flavors and advertised that each can contained all the nutrients of a whole meal. Even Eli went on the Metrecal diet in his late teens, but when he complained to my mother that he wasn't losing weight, she discovered that he was drinking several cans of Metrecal a day in addition to eating three full meals.

As the 1960s began, the goods sold at Zabar's were simple, traditional, and pretty much what my grandfather had been stocking in the 1940s. This was what the public wanted to buy, and Saul had been happy to spend his first decade of being in charge not innovating but simply trying hard to maintain the formidable standards that had been established by his father. Running from one store to another was particularly grueling. Saul wanted to do one thing and do it well, and so as the lease on each of the storefronts came up for renewal (in one case, a fire caused severe damage), my uncle would let the store go, against my father's objections—none of which really carried all that much weight with Saul. Although he was still a co-owner and assisting his brother as much as he could, my father was working full-time as an attorney and wasn't willing to give that up to keep all of the stores going.

By the early 1960s, Saul was focusing his energies on one store: Zabar's on Eightieth Street and Broadway. And now he had the time to do something he had been thinking about: adding new offerings to the old classics. Business administration may not have been his forte, but my uncle did have a sense that the gastronomic times were changing and that what his customers wanted was about to change, too.

Zabar's appetizing counter in the 1960s. This was what I remember the appetizing counter looking like when I was a girl. Even then, the Zabar's style was a cornucopia of offerings heaped together in a haphazard fashion.

Saul had no intention of altering the traditional appetizing and delicatessen that Zabar's was known for. He simply added other gourmet items, many of them previously unavailable in the United States. He knew, for example, that his customers would enjoy high-quality bread to go with their smoked fish, so he began to stock a diverse collection of artisanal breads. While most Americans were eating packaged Wonder Bread, Zabar's offered twenty-five varieties of freshly baked bread—many of them whole grain or prepared without preservatives—that were made by small bakeries in the Bronx, Brooklyn, New Jersey, and Philadelphia. Zabar's now sold French bread by the foot, flourless soy loaves, black Russian rye bread, German pumpernickel, and Polish rye bread. And, of course, different varieties of bagels and bialys.

Saul's timing was perfect. An increasing number of Americans were beginning to travel to Europe as commercial transatlantic flights became more available, and when those people returned, they wanted to buy the foods they'd been introduced to overseas. And so Saul began to import a range of condiments—all kinds of oils, vinegars, mustards, honeys, and spices—from England, France, Ireland, Italy, Australia, and the Netherlands.

Saul had another reason for all this updating: he was hoping to sell Zabar's and wanted to make the package as attractive as possible to potential buyers. He had given running the store his best shot, but despite the enticements of the expanded gourmet offerings, the profit margins were extremely narrow and expenses were still higher than income: Zabar's was losing $200,000 a year. Stressed by a divorce from Rosalie and ready for a life change, in 1961, Saul put Zabar's on the market for $565,000. No buyers appeared, and there was nothing for Saul to do but carry on. But my uncle and my father realized that they could not keep Zabar's going by themselves. So they appealed to Murray Klein, who had left their employ in 1957, to come back and help them turn the business around.

Murray had lived a harsh and tumultuous life. He was born in 1923 in Ukraine, near the Romanian border. World War II turned his world upside down. While he was a teenager attending a trade school in the Soviet Union, his parents and five siblings were sent to Nazi concentration camps, where they all perished. Because he had destroyed his identity papers, Murray was sent to a Soviet labor camp in Siberia. Once there, he pretended to be ill, was sent to a hospital, and then made his escape. Ever an entrepreneur, Murray survived by selling bread on the black market in Siberia, until the threat of arrest for his illegal activities spurred an escape to Tashkent, where he remained until the end of the war. His next stop was a displaced persons camp in Rome, which had been set up in the then vacant film studio Cinecittà. There he joined the Irgun, the underground Jewish paramilitary organization, and helped smuggle arms from Europe to the Jews who were battling the British army in Mandatory Palestine. Those activities led to his arrest and imprisonment by the British, but, once again, Murray found a way out, this time by staging a hunger strike that led to his release. Eventually, after Murray had endured roughly a decade of war and displacement, his cousin Aaron Klein found his name on a Red Cross list of war refugees and sponsored his immigration to America in 1950. Shortly after his arrival, he began working for the Zabars, first as a delivery and stock man and eventually as the manager of one of the Broadway stores. He left in 1957 to run his own businesses, including a hardware store.

Saul and Stanley succeeded in getting Murray to agree to return to Zabar's, where he was put in charge of the day-to-day operations, opening up the store every morning at 6:00 a.m. Three years later, he became a full one-third partner. A stocky, balding man with close-cropped graying hair, heavy-lidded green eyes, and a thick Russian Yiddish accent, Murray often sardonically referred to himself as a "peasant," or as one of the "proletariat," in contrast to the Zabars, whom he called "Jewish royalty."

But, ultimately, it was working-class Murray who rescued Zabar's from financial ruin and transformed the store into what it is today. He was a retail savant with a talent for both buying and selling food and appliances at the lowest possible prices. If the price of a product rose to too high a level, he dropped the item, even when it was in demand. Instead of creating a spare, elegant, and luxurious atmosphere, Murray stocked the store to its limits, hanging pots and pans, strings of garlic, salamis, and teakettles from the ceiling

Zabar's appetizing counter, 1971. Murray intentionally created a bazaar-like atmosphere with housewares hanging from the ceiling. (MICHAEL GOLD FOR *THE NEW YORK TIMES*)

to create the sense of a chaotic yet exciting food bazaar. "If I walk out onto Zabar's floor and I can see my shoes," he would say, "it's not busy enough."

Saul's prescient expansion into imported and artisanal offerings, combined with Murray's astute management and salesmanship, occurred at a pivotal time in food history, keeping Zabar's ahead of the curve during a time in which Americans' taste in food was undergoing a revolutionary change. First Lady Jacqueline Kennedy sparked a national interest in sophisticated French cuisine by hiring the French chef René Verdon for the White House kitchen in 1961. Perhaps the most influential event in the growing fascination with French food was the 1963 debut of Julia Child's televised cooking show, *The French Chef*. My immediate family had never been to France (they'd actually never been anywhere in Europe), and *The French Chef* was a groundbreaking introduction to a new and exciting cuisine and culture. Inspired by the series, my mother took a break from chicken baked in mushroom soup and tackled complicated recipes like beef Wellington from Julia Child's cookbook *Mastering the Art of French Cooking*, which had been published to considerable acclaim in 1961. My mother and my aunt Carole, Saul's second wife, took cooking lessons from a Viennese woman named Mrs. Simon in her house in Kew Gardens, Queens, where they learned how to make a delicious nut torte. My parents and Saul and Carole also spent occasional weekends at an inn in Pine Plains, New York, called Monblason, where the French owner/chef Charles Virion whipped up fabulous feasts. In January 1968, my parents, together with Murray and his wife, Edith, finally made it to Europe, eating their way across the Atlantic on the S.S. *France,* where there was unlimited caviar at dinner.

I, too, was swept up by the thrill of French food and became particularly enamored of French pastry. My ideal was the strawberry tart log at Patisserie Dumas in Manhattan. It was a rectangle of buttery, feather-light mille-feuille pastry spread with a layer of silky crème anglaise and topped with plump, lightly jam-glazed strawberries. It was heavenly, and worth dealing with the imposing cashier who glowered at the customers from her perch behind the cash register.

By the mid-1960s, Zabar's had become a fashionable place to shop for both gourmet offerings and traditional Jewish appetizing and delicatessen. Actors, musicians, and intellectuals who lived and worked nearby, as well as neighborhood residents, congregated at Zabar's on the weekends to socialize while stocking up for Saturday and Sunday brunch. The store was open until midnight from Sunday through Friday and until 1:00 a.m. on Saturday, and when the RKO movie theater on Eighty-First Street and the Loew's on Eighty-Third Street let out at about 11:00 p.m., a surge of moviegoers filled the store, along with Broadway theatergoers coming up from midtown. For longtime customer Howard Sage, Friday and Saturday nights didn't feel complete without a late-night rendezvous with friends at Zabar's. Around midnight, he recalled, the store was "festive, luxurious, warming, intense, and tasty. And that's without even mentioning the fulfilling moments of having a knish to take home, pickles to savor, and even some tantalizing breakfast tidbits for Sunday morning."

The ritual of Zabar's Sunday brunch was both a joy and a challenge for my friend Laura Kaminsky and her two sisters when they were preteens in the 1960s. Every Sunday, the family dissected world events in their apartment on West Seventy-Ninth Street over bagels and smoked salmon, matjes herring, salamis, Gruyère, and a big plate of crudités. "Our parents were insistent that my sisters and I be aware of the world in which we lived," Laura recalled. "We slogged through the newspapers all week, keeping track of the emerging stories, anticipating, with more than a little dread, The Sunday News Discussion. It was about learning how to defend one's thoughts. The student protests of 1968, Vietnam and Cambodia, Biafra, Israel and Egypt—all of this was avidly discussed at our Zabar's-laden table as another schmear of cream cheese was spread on a slice of pumpernickel bread. It was all very intimate, passionate, and tasty. To this day our family goes to Zabar's, buys our favorite things, and gathers around the table to debate the news of the day." Laura's compulsory topical news discussions over Zabar's brunch paid off: she's now a composer of chamber operas that are informed by current events and contemporary issues.

Zabar's had even amassed enough cachet in the 1960s to appear in newspaper gossip columns. In Joe Kaliff's nationally syndicated column about show business personalities, "Magic Carpet Over Broadway," Kaliff revealed a definite pickle fixation. He described Greta Garbo as a sour-pickle addict who ordered them by the keg from Zabar's and also wrote about when "Zabar's, the fancy appetizer store on upper Broadway, was thrown into a turmoil the other day, when actor Van Johnson lost his signet ring in the sour-pickle barrel." (It's quite unlikely that any of this actually occurred.)

Murray's day-to-day management and interaction with the customers freed Saul to do what he loved. In addition to selecting the very best smoked fish for Zabar's, beginning in 1966, my uncle revolutionized the way the store bought and sold coffee. In the old days, coffee beans arrived at the docks in downtown Manhattan adjacent to the coffee district on Front Street, near the Fulton Fish Market. The brokers went down to the docks and bought barrels of coffee beans for their customers. Then the brokers sent the beans to a coffee roaster, and when they were ready, a trucker delivered the roasted beans to stores such as Zabar's. The retailers were not in any way involved in the procuring, evaluating, or roasting of the coffee beans. They just hoped the end product would taste good.

Saul was one of the first gourmet purveyors to customize roasting coffee; what results from this process is known today as artisanal, small-batch coffee. To learn this craft, he had apprenticed himself in the early 1960s to White Coffee Corporation in Long Island City, a roaster that supplied mainly restaurants and hotels with a high-quality, all-arabica blend. Every day for a year, he'd arrived for two hours of roasting and cupping sessions. Once he understood what was required to source good coffee, he began to buy directly hundreds of pounds of coffee for the store. After he completed his apprenticeship, Saul persuaded White Coffee to expand their offerings with such varieties as Kenya AA, Tanzanian Peaberry, Jamaican Blue Mountain, Hawaiian Kona, and Guatemalan Antigua.

Saul then instituted the Zabar's coffee process, which has continued to this day. It begins with his procurement of small samples of green beans (the beans' original color, before they are roasted) from importers to roast, cup, and taste. Once he approves a sample, he orders between 125 and 250 bags from that shipment, each weighing between 125 and 150 pounds, which will be stored in the Zabar's warehouse. Generally, Zabar's keeps 75,000 to 100,000 pounds of coffee beans in storage at any given time.

When the beans are delivered, Saul roasts test batches of what will eventually become his own special stock, watching constantly to determine by eye when a batch reaches the right color. Most coffee roasters prefer a dark roast because it's easier to achieve, but to Saul's taste, the right color is a lighter brown. When roasting light, Saul says, "we're riding the razor's edge. Any little slip gives you a cut." Even a second either way makes a difference in the way the roast comes out. According to Saul, a light roast provides subtleties. "It's like orchestral music," he says. "If everyone is playing loud, you can't hear those nuances."

Next, Saul created a procedure for tasting the roasted coffee to

Saul roasting and tasting coffee, sometime in the 1970s. He's still doing it today, at age ninety-three. (COPYRIGHT © ZABAR'S AND COMPANY, INC. ALL RIGHTS RESERVED.)

ensure that the test batches were up to his standard. On a revolving table in his office, ten to twelve bags of roasted beans are arranged in a circle, each bag with notations on the details of preparation, such as the temperature and duration of the roast. In front of each bag is a rectangular metal tray holding coffee that has been ground from the beans in that bag. And in front of each tray is a small ceramic bowl (it's not really a cup, even though the process is referred to as "cupping"). From each tray, the same amount of ground coffee is measured and placed into its bowl, and then boiling water is poured over the ground coffee. Next, Saul "breaks the coffee," which means he stirs the coffee in each bowl with a spoon and then sniffs its aroma. When the coffee reaches medium temperature, he slurps the coffee in each bowl with a spoon, so that it's combined with as much air as possible as it washes over his tongue. Then he quickly spits the coffee out into a spittoon. After the coffee has cooled a bit, he goes through the same cupping process again, to evaluate the coffee for acidity, body, and roast level. Saul approves the roast for each test batch of beans for each variety of coffee before the hundreds of bags in storage are roasted. Zabar's roasts coffee once a week in roasters that hold six hundred pounds of beans, just enough to supply customers in the store and by mail order. This means that Zabar's beans are always fresh, and ready to be ground by either the staff or the customers into Zabar's legendary coffee.

While Saul was tending to the coffee and the smoked fish and Murray was refashioning Zabar's into a lively culinary emporium, Eli was working as a night manager in the store while attending Columbia University's School of General Studies during the day. When he graduated in 1967, Eli felt he was ready for a major role

Stanley, Saul, Murray, and Eli, sometime in the late 1960s, before Eli went out on his own. (COPYRIGHT © ZABAR'S AND COMPANY, INC. ALL RIGHTS RESERVED.)

at Zabar's. His brothers and Murray disagreed. They thought it was too soon to give him the full partnership he was seeking. Eli felt rejected, but it was more a matter of Saul, Stanley, and Murray thinking that Eli needed more experience in running a store, and their feeling that Zabar's was at that time too small to take on a fourth partner. Frustrated, Eli left Zabar's to go out on his own. Years later, Eli conceded that he had not been denied something that was rightfully due him at the time. Contrary to a prevailing myth, Eli and his brothers remain very close. Even after he left, Eli still asked Saul and Stanley for advice. When Eli opened his first store, E.A.T., my father was discreetly watching in the wings, making sure Eli did not get in over his head. Eventually, Saul and Eli pooled their buying power to get the best prices from suppliers. At Zabar family holiday gatherings, the three brothers still huddle together and talk shop.

While Zabar's was becoming a gourmet legend, I was living the life of a 1960s elementary-school kid at P.S. 139 in Rego Park, Queens, devouring fairy tales and British children's books and harboring a desire to live in a medieval castle. At one point, I'd decided that I had been switched at birth with one of Queen Elizabeth's children, and that once my true identity was proven, I would go live in Buckingham Palace. My father was unimpressed by my desire to become a member of the British royal family. "To me you're already a princess, my Jewish princess," he'd say. And I had to admit that on special days when my father took me to spend a Saturday with Grandma Lilly, I did feel like a true princess.

My grandmother's supreme joy and greatest act of love was to feed her family and friends, whether she prepared the meal herself or hosted everyone at a restaurant. (She always made twice as much food as she would need, "just in case.") Grandma Lilly's love of food meant that our Saturdays together followed a delicious ritual. We generally started with lunch at Schrafft's, on Broadway between Eighty-Second and Eighty-Third Streets, on the street level of a two-story building that looked a bit like a wedding cake, with garlands and swags on the outside. A large iron-and-glass marquee overhanging a glass storefront with an enticing view of chocolates and other confections welcomed us. Beyond the candy counters was the high-ceilinged sunken restaurant. To me it was the height of elegance—subdued lighting, white tablecloths, waiters and waitresses in uniforms—especially when compared with the pizza place or the Jewish deli near my elementary school. I could order whatever I wanted. I always got a Coke or a ginger ale, and Grandma Lilly always asked for a cup of Sanka. "Hot, make sure it is very hot!" she'd say to the waiter. Sometimes it wasn't hot enough and she sent it back. We gossiped and laughed as we ate our tuna on rye (for Grandma) and turkey club (for me). She thought I was so smart, so pretty, so stylish. I was the girl child my grandmother never had, and I basked in her enthusiasm and attention.

We took dessert, especially ice cream desserts, very seriously. Both of us were chubby, but fortunately, Grandma Lilly didn't know or care that my doctor and my mother thought I should restrict my sweets. It was always a hard choice between the chocolate ice cream soda with coffee ice cream and the coffee ice cream sundae with hot fudge sauce. We agreed that coffee ice cream was the best.

Lunch was only the prelude. Once the meal was done, we sometimes stopped by the Bartons candy store, where I had a special affection for the almond butter crunch chocolate squares. Grandma Lilly said they got stuck in her dentures, but she bought a small box for me to take home.

Our next stop was Rappaport's children's store, to buy a party dress for an upcoming family event or a classmate's birthday party. My mother had excellent taste and definite opinions about what clothes were appropriate for young girls, but Grandma Lilly was happy with whatever I chose. And it didn't matter how much it cost. Sometimes we went to Indian Walk to buy a pair of patent leather Mary Janes or ballerina flats to coordinate with the new dress, and a pair of clunky-looking laced-up walking shoes for Grandma Lilly. At Levy Brothers stationers and toy store, I could choose a toy for myself and one for my brother. She was never too impatient to discuss all of the pluses and minuses of the various options. I usually selected an art-related project for myself and a model airplane kit for David.

The only thing left to do after that was walk a couple of blocks to Grandma Lilly's apartment at 118 Riverside Drive and relax until my father arrived, or stroll down Broadway to the store to meet up with him for the ride home. Either way, it was the end of a perfect day.

Aside from our occasional jaunts on the Upper West Side, most of our time together took place during the summer in Mohegan Colony, where Grandma Lilly was the Colony's most vivacious resident. At parties in New York City, her exuberant greetings to other guests always included an invitation to Mohegan.

The cottage my grandparents had bought decades earlier was now the site of many family meals and celebrations for both the older and younger generations. Whenever my family arrived in her driveway on a Friday night for Shabbat dinner, we could immediately smell the delicious aromas wafting from her kitchen. We never bothered going to the front door; entering via the side door on the enclosed porch brought us right into her kitchen. "I have chicken, I have soup," she'd say as she greeted us. "There's chopped liver and stuffed cabbage and a pot roast in the oven." After we said the blessings over the candles, wine, and challah, Grandpa Louis Chartoff sat quietly at the table while Grandma Lilly ricocheted almost breathlessly between the dining table and the kitchen. "A small glass of juice?" she would say. "Perhaps another helping of chicken soup?" "Lilly, why don't you sit down and eat with us?" my mother would ask. But my grandmother was too intent on making sure we were all happy with our meal. For dessert, she liked to make thumbprint butter cookies with depressed centers that were filled with jam. But in an uncharacteristic bow to nutritional concerns, she often left out one ingredient in the hopes of making the cookies healthier. Sometimes she would forgo the salt, other times the sugar. One time she didn't include the butter! We would beg her to keep to the original recipe, which produced delicious cookies. (See the recipe on page 121.)

At some point during the meal, Grandma Lilly would often exclaim, "I love having my family for Shabbat! The important thing is to be together." But then she'd become pensive and say, "Why isn't Saul here? Where is Eli? I wish they were here, too." At this, my parents, David, Sandy, Grandpa Louis, and I would look at one another and think, "Well, what are we, chopped liver?" It would never have occurred to her that this made all of us feel a bit undervalued. The physical presence of her entire family was the only thing that soothed her intermittent anxiety and made her feel more secure in her adopted country. She'd left Russia expecting to see her parents when she returned to Ostropolia in a few years' time, but instead she never saw her family again. No wonder she wanted all of us to be as physically near to her as often as possible.

When I was very young, my parents rented houses during the summer in Lido Beach and Fire Island on Long Island. My grandmother missed us at Mohegan, and when I turned six, she bought the cottage on the acre adjacent to her house and gave it to my father as a present. The only problem was that no one told my mother until it was a fait accompli. Understandably upset that she hadn't been consulted, my mother made my father promise that we would not spend every summer in Mohegan and would continue to rent houses at the beach on Long Island. He agreed, but in actual fact my parents never went anywhere but to Mohegan for the summer. They are now among the few second-home owners in the Colony, which has become an affordable commuter suburb for New York City.

When we were spending summers there in the 1960s, Mohegan was a modest middle-class summer community of primarily Jewish families from the city, but the Colony had begun as a utopian cooperative in 1923. An anarchist and progressive educator named Harry Kelly purchased 450 acres from the Baron de Hirsch Fund. He then distributed the land among members of the Mohegan Colony. The main purpose of the community was to establish a model progressive school in 1924, but ideological divisions among its anarchist, communist, socialist, and libertarian members resulted in the closing of the school in 1941. In 1952, Mohegan was reincorporated as the Mohegan Colony Association, with a focus on community maintenance and upkeep, but it continued to promote cultural events and progressive ideals.

The Colony did retain a few holdovers from its radical past. The two-story house on Forest Lane down the block from Grandma Lilly's cottage had once belonged to Rudolf Rocker, who, according to my mother, was a famous anarchist. Most of the community's anarchists and communists were long gone from Mohegan, but my friend Ruthy Rotholz remembers going with her sister Susie to the house across the street from their home whenever they thought their neighbor was having a party, in search of candy or other treats. They were always welcomed. It was only years later that Ruthy realized that she and Susie were crashing meetings of the elderly members of the Mohegan chapter of the American Communist Party.

In the summer of 1960, my brother and I found out that Pete Seeger was scheduled to sing folk songs at Mohegan Colony's very own Martha Ginsberg Pavilion. We loved listening to Seeger's records at home, and we were beside ourselves at the prospect of seeing him live. But when we arrived for the concert, I observed families I had never seen before walking back and forth with picket signs reading GO HOME, COMMUNISTS! and PETE SEEGER IS A PINKO! My mother explained that some people who lived outside of the Colony didn't want Pete Seeger to sing there because they disliked anyone they thought was a communist. We walked past the picketers, pretending they weren't there, but their rude behavior shocked my six-year-old self. If they didn't like him or his politics, I thought they should just stay home and let others enjoy his music.

Our summers and weekends in Mohegan gave me additional opportunities to spend time alone with Grandma Lilly. Many an evening after dinner at my house, I would pass through the hedge of pine trees that separated our properties and head straight to her bedroom, where she was usually watching the news or a news feature on television. "Lorki!" she'd exclaim. "Come see Golda Meir on TV! Can you imagine a woman is the prime minister of Israel? Such a strong, brilliant woman!" My grandmother was an enthusiastic supporter of Israel and prided herself on selling more Israel bonds than anyone else in her chapter of the Pioneer Women organization. Grandma Lilly viewed selling bonds as a competitive sport. When she arrived at a gathering of people on my parents' porch in Mohegan, everyone there knew they would not be able to leave without purchasing a bond in support of Israel.

Sometimes, as a special treat, I was allowed to sleep over in my

Grandma Lilly dancing the hora with her stepdaughter
Dr. Evelyn Chartoff Gaynor, at my bat mitzvah reception
in 1967. Lilly lit up the room at social gatherings.
(ZABAR FAMILY COLLECTION)

grandparents' guest room. At bedtime, Grandma Lilly sat with me as I dozed off (or, as she said, "went *schluffen*"), singing in Yiddish the Russian Jewish love song "Tumbalalaika," or telling me stories about her childhood in Ostropolia. On nights when I didn't sleep over, she always reminded me to "take a searchlight!" to guide me "through the bushes." Even after decades in America, my grandmother sometimes had difficulty coming up with the right English word and often spoke as if she were translating in her head from Russian or Yiddish.

There were many parties in Mohegan, and one of the most memorable was Eli's wedding, in 1969, when I was fifteen. My father was the best man, and I was thrilled to be the bridesmaid.

Eli and his fiancée, Abbie Wagman, planned a summer afternoon celebration on Lilly's lawn. Abbie, a talented interior designer and artist, was very particular about aesthetics, right down to instructing me to wear white so that I would fit in with her color scheme. She adhered to the "less is more" 1960s design principle, except when it came to cost, and in that respect was a good match for Eli, who also had simple but impeccable taste. His birthday gifts were often items that were culturally or aesthetically beyond me at the time, such as Bob Dylan's first record album, which he gave me when I was seven, and a gorgeous cherry-red Mark Cross leather portfolio, which I received from him when I was in junior high. I also remember his presenting my parents with a beautiful ceramic plate painted by Picasso that he'd picked up in Vallauris while on a bicycle trip through France.

So it came as no surprise that this couple had very particular plans for their nuptials. The menu for the afternoon wedding, Eli and Abbie informed Grandma Lilly, would be caviar, strawberries and cream, wedding cake, and champagne.

Grandma Lilly was aghast. Not only was the food not at all Jewish, it was also far too sparse. At a Jewish wedding, guests expect a full meal after the ceremony. "Eli," she declared, "I cannot invite my crowd, who will have traveled all the way here from Manhattan and Brooklyn, to a wedding where they will eat nothing more than hors d'oeuvres. They'll be hungry!"

But Eli said that the menu was not negotiable.

The wedding day was bright and sunny. Eli wore a blue blazer, an open-collared button-down shirt, and loafers without socks; Abbie looked chic in a simple form-fitting V-necked white silk minidress and low-heeled matching Italian pumps. The rabbi performed the wedding service on the lawn. Afterward, the guests drank the champagne and nibbled on the elegant but quickly warming repast while a band played songs by The Lovin' Spoonful.

I was munching on strawberries and feeling very sophisticated in a white halter dress and platform sandals that I'd chosen myself when I noticed a strange pattern of behavior on the part of some of the guests. My grandmother's friends seemed to be excusing themselves frequently to use the bathroom in the house. I decided to see for myself what was going on. There in the dinette was a long table filled with roast chickens, bowls piled high with coleslaw and potato salad, loaves of sliced bread, plates of butter, and piles of cookies. Grandma Lilly somehow managed to sneak all this food from the store into her house so that she could save face with her friends without interfering with the incomprehensibly gentile menu that had been selected by the bride and groom. As for me, I'd enjoyed Abbie and Eli's elegant tidbits, but now I happily helped myself to an excellent lunch.

Many years later, at a charitable event held at Kurland · Zabar, an antiques gallery on the Upper East Side I used to co-own with Catherine Kurland, I saw a gray-bearded man who had not purchased a ticket scarfing down the Scotch salmon hors d'oeuvres. When I politely asked him to leave, he insisted that he was entitled to be there because he was the rabbi who had married Eli and Abbie. I suppose he felt he was owed a meal, despite the fact that his marital blessings were not successful; Eli and Abbie's marriage ended sixteen years after their wedding in Mohegan.

Eli Zabar's Thumbprint Cookies

Inspired by Lilly Zabar's recipe
Edited and tested by Monita Buchwald

Thumbprint cookies probably originated in Eastern Europe. They are versatile in that they can accommodate a variety of fruit fillings, but my grandmother chose to experiment with the pastry portion, often leaving out one essential ingredient or another in her hapless quest to create a "nutritious" cookie. She so enjoyed watching us eat them that I forced myself to consume many a tasteless cookie after Shabbat dinner because I knew they were made with love. Fortunately, my uncle Eli is a talented baker and has created a delicious version based on Grandma Lilly's recipe—but with all the necessary ingredients present and accounted for.

MAKES ABOUT 42 COOKIES

INGREDIENTS

8 tablespoons (1 stick) salted
   butter, at room temperature
⅓ cup sugar
1 large egg yolk

1 cup all-purpose flour
½ cup good-quality jam, such as
   raspberry jam with seeds, or
   apricot

DIRECTIONS

1. Using an electric mixer, cream the butter and sugar until pale and fluffy. Add the egg yolk, mix again, and scrape down the sides of the bowl. Add the flour last and mix until combined.
2. Form the dough into a round disk and refrigerate for at least 2 hours or overnight.
3. Preheat the oven to 350°F.

4. Remove the dough from the refrigerator, let stand for a few minutes to soften, and place on a lightly floured surface. Roll out the dough until it's about ½ inch thick. Use a 1-inch cookie cutter to cut the dough into rounds. Reroll the scraps. Alternatively, you can form 1-inch balls.

5. Arrange the rounds or balls on two parchment-lined cookie sheets. Press a finger into the center of each cookie. It doesn't actually have to be your thumb: Grandma Lilly used her pointer. That indentation is for the jam.

6. Put the jam in a sealable plastic bag and cut off one bottom corner. Use it as you would a pastry bag to pipe a drop (about ½ teaspoon) of jam into the center of each cookie.

7. Bake for about 12 minutes, until the edges are golden—you do not want them to become too dark.

8. Cool on a rack, then store in an airtight container. These cookies keep well for about a week.

Smoked whitefish: moist, flaky, and subtly sweet.

Nova salmon:
cold-smoked, silky, and mild

Belly lox:
bold, brine-cured, and salty

Scotch-cured Nova Salmon:
lean and medium smoky

Double-smoked salmon:
lean and smoky

Gravlax:
sugar- and salt-cured, topped with dill

Peppered nova:
peppery and garlicky

Hand-sliced smoked salmon. (JUAN C. LOPEZ ESPANTALEON/COPYRIGHT
© ZABAR'S AND COMPANY, INC. ALL RIGHTS RESERVED.)

Beef salami; deli knishes; Zabar's signature sourdough rye bread; hand-sliced pastrami and corned beef; mini knishes; sour pickles; deli mustard.

Zabar's "Holiday Any Day Cheese Box": (Counterclockwise, from bottom right) *French Chaource; Les Trois Petits Cochons* (imported petits toasts); *Spanish Queso Leonora; Italian Cacio di Bosco al Tartufo; Spanish walnuts in lemon honey; English Stilton.* (STEPHANIE WILLOUGHBY/COPYRIGHT © ZABAR'S AND COMPANY, INC. ALL RIGHTS RESERVED.)

Chicken soup with matzoh ball. See page 31 for Lilly Zabar's recipe.

Potato latkes. See page 67 for Lilly Zabar's recipe.

Zabar's coffee and the store's iconic mug.

Chocolate and raisin rugelach.

Mini black-and-white cookies.

Cinnamon and chocolate babkas.

Zabar's "Don't Be Homesick Gift Crate," one of the many gift baskets and boxes offered by the store. (JUAN C. LOPEZ ESPANTALEON/COPYRIGHT

8

The Epicurean Emporium Expands, 1970–84

AROUND 1970, MY FATHER LEFT THE LAW TO WORK FULL-TIME AT Zabar's. Whenever he would close a difficult deal, there would be no praise for his hard work and legal acumen—the participants wanted to talk only about Zabar's. He thought it would be more fulfilling to return to the store, and it was. Under Murray Klein's administration, Zabar's had become profitable. There was now room for another active partner.

With his undergraduate degree in business administration, his law degree, and his LLM in tax law, my father focused on the financial end of Zabar's. He was the one who dealt with the ins and outs of employment regulations, health insurance, and pension plans. But he also wanted a role in selecting the store's provisions and decided to create his own fiefdom in the meat and deli department. This was a man who had never cooked anything but eggs or eaten pork in any form, yet he dove headfirst into sourcing and developing innovative meat products. The Zabar family mantra is that we can achieve anything as long as we do the research and persevere. Prior experience is not a prerequisite for success.

With his newfound purpose, Stanley worked alongside the chef at Zabar's, experimenting with ingredients to come up with new recipes for the deli counter. His other accomplice was Harold Horowytz, the large, jovial manager of the department, who arrived at Zabar's in 1972. My father was soon bringing home a variety of products and prepared dishes for us to test. One month we ate endless racks of New Zealand lamb; another month he brought home a stream of main courses incorporating the leftover carcasses of the smoked turkey sold in the deli department. Generally, we welcomed these tastings, but I did eventually tire of the smoked turkey. I haven't eaten any since.

Sometimes my father arrived with some special samples outside his usual purview; anyone who happened to be around would join in our taste tests. When I was in high school, we spent several very enjoyable weeks sampling beluga, osetra, and sevruga caviar. My friend Wendy Miller was pleasantly shocked when I offered her caviar for breakfast one morning after a sleepover. Of all the foods we tested, caviar was my favorite, and I developed a passion for the large black shiny beluga fish eggs that tasted like the sea.

For some reason, at Zabar's baked goods were part of the deli domain. One time, we were obliged to evaluate ten different fruit pies, and my friend Linda Kartoz listened in astonishment as my ten-year-old sister, Sandy, eloquently compared the weight and textures of the various crusts. Another time, in a foray into frozen foods, my father, my friend Claudia Kane, and I decided to check out the offerings at a local Baskin-Robbins ice cream store, as the brand was becoming famous for its "31 flavors." In single-minded research-and-development mode, we purchased and tasted at least twenty different flavors in ice cream cones, while the other customers in the store looked on in disbelief. Claudia and I were tasked with trying all the chocolate offerings, because my father doesn't eat chocolate anything. He and I were already Häagen-Dazs enthusiasts, and we felt the Baskin-Robbins flavors tasted artificial, their texture insufficiently creamy in comparison. Claudia was less critical than we were, but she happily volunteered for any other Zabar's taste tests that might be in the offing.

My father's efforts paid off. In her column in *New York* magazine, restaurant and food critic Gael Greene called Zabar's meat department "a hotbed of creativity." Under my father's and Harold's aegis, the deli counter offered an astounding variety. There were ducklings filled with stuffing made from ground apples and bread crumbs, juicy meat loaf, lip-smacking veal ribs, mouthwatering corned beef, and several types of hams—honey, molasses, apple, and hickory. There was also Black Forest bacon, salamis, meat sausages from mild to red-hot, and liverwurst. One day, my father purchased a hickory smoker and told Harold to experiment.

Harold went all out. In the Zabar's cramped kitchen, which turned out five tons of food a week, he smoked just about everything: ribs, pork, chicken, duck, brisket, shell steak, prime rib, turkey, lamb, and rabbit.

As the deli department was beginning to expand its horizons, another major marketing development occurred. In 1972, Elliot Schneider, an Upper West Sider and principal of a graphic design and branding firm, made a cold call on Saul to see if he could do anything for Zabar's. Saul showed Elliot an old piece of Zabar's publicity with the name Zabar's appearing within a circle and hired him to design a shopping bag. Elliot straightened out the circular format and enhanced the Gothic-looking lettering. He also added a list of the store's offerings in simple block type and an old-fashioned illustration of groceries in barrels that he found in a book of clip art. He flipped through the Pantone color catalog and chose orange for the logo (because it felt right, he said), adding it to Zabar's existing brown-and-white color scheme. Then he extended the graphic branding to appetizing and deli wrapping paper, plastic food containers, T-shirts, baseball caps, coffee mugs, and canvas totes. Little did Elliot know that his design would become a world-famous icon. A Zabar's shopping bag circa 1992 is in the collection of the Cooper Hewitt, Smithsonian Design Museum in New York City.

Those were the less frenetic days, when you could submit a grocery list in person or over the phone, and a couple of hours later pick up all your items at the cash register, neatly packed in shopping bags with your name on them. One time, I put in an order that included peasant bread and came home to discover a roasted pheasant in my bag! I was mildly disappointed that I didn't get the bread but amazed to learn that Zabar's offered pheasant.

Other customers became irate when an unanticipated ingredient showed up in their bag. My father once received a letter from a customer who was upset at finding some stray caraway seeds in a container of Zabar's cream cheese. As evidence, she had taped three seeds to the letter. "Thank you so much for your letter," my father wrote back. "We were looking all over for those seeds."

Stanley had found new energy in being his own boss and joy

in the ongoing improvements in the store's deli department and financial operations. But his work persona remained one of high anxiety combined with a distressing lack of punctuality. He always insisted that the latter was simply his way of operating on universally accepted "Jewish time."

When I was a freshman at Barnard in 1971–72 and living at home in Queens, I sometimes hitched a ride home from school with my father. Inevitably, I would arrive at Zabar's at the appointed time and locate my father, brow furrowed and frowning, racing down the stairs from his office on one of his periodic visits to the main floor, his eyes intently tracking the activity around him to see if the deli counter needed another clerk or if the lines at the cash registers were backing up. This was my father in work mode, anticipating and averting another impending retail disaster.

"Another ten minutes," he would say as he dashed past me, so I would spend my time wandering around the store, picking up an apple to munch on or chatting with Sam Cohen behind the appetizing counter, catching up with him about his children. Then I'd check in again. *"Another ten minutes,"* my father would implore. I'd go next door to Beck's Drugstore and do a turn around the exterior entranceway, following the circular mosaic pattern. I'd examine the garishly painted wooden Native American statue standing in front of the United Cigar Store on the corner. Then I'd walk up and down Broadway. By the time my father was finally ready to leave, I'd calculated that if I had left for home directly from school and taken the three trains that would get me to Rego Park, I could have already been there. As we walked across the street to the garage, he turned to me and said, "Never go into retail, Lori! You have to be there all the time just to keep people on track. Unless an owner is around to solve problems, it's a disaster."

That was my work father. When we were at home, he was another person entirely, one who was delighted to spend extended periods of time with me and my siblings. He wanted to know about my classes, my plans for a summer internship or a trip abroad. At home, he said things like, "The world is your oyster! You can do anything you want professionally."

All of the Zabars are anxious—Saul and Eli and their kids, my dad, my siblings, and I. I've always thought it started with the Zabarkas and the Teitelbaums in the antisemitic atmosphere of Ostropolia, and that my grandparents' anxiety and fear of separation just got passed down to succeeding generations. It's something I myself have had to work on, and in recent years, it's been interesting to see how the fourth generation of Zabars deals with this peculiar legacy. When my son Henry's sixth-grade teacher asked everyone in the class to state their family's motto, Henry told me that "I gave them Grandpa Stanley's motto: 'If it's close, it's good.'"

My father certainly lived by that. My parents moved back to the Upper West Side from Queens in 1973, and ever since, my father's world has been contained within a ten-block radius. He lives around the corner from the store, one block from where he grew up and one block from his elementary school. Almost all of his commercial real estate investments, each one co-owned with family members, are nearby. My brother, my sister, and I live within his ten-block radius, as do Saul and his wife. Grandma Lilly's apartment was just a few blocks away. Only Eli, who resides on the other side of Central Park, managed to make it out of the Zabar shtetl.

The other way the Zabars stave off anxiety and fear of separation is through relentless hard work—another legacy that has been bequeathed to us by Louis and Lilly. Each of their grandchildren and great-grandchildren has worked at Zabar's at some point in their lives. My several turns at the store included a stint behind the counter on Friday afternoons during my freshman year of college; my job was mainly slicing cheese and grinding coffee. I could never understand why the cheese department included baklava, the prodigiously sweet, layered phyllo pastry that was filled with chopped nuts and honey that dripped out of the sides. I always prayed that no one would ask for it, because no matter how hard I tried to wipe it off, the sticky mess clung to my fingers for the rest of the day, picking up stray bits of the coffee I was grinding.

Many of my customers were elderly people from the neighborhood who wanted nothing more than two slices of Jarlsberg or a smidgen of pot cheese. I was under strict orders from Murray Klein not to sell less than a quarter pound of anything, but all of my attempts at explaining the store's policy were fruitless. "I'm

*My brother, David (in a Zabar's hat), and me, selling
bagels, lox, and novie at an event outside the American
Museum of Natural History, 1972. Working at Zabar's during
school holidays and summers is a given for each generation
of young Zabars.*

all alone," an elderly lady would protest. "I can't eat such a huge
amount by myself." I would then try to talk these customers into
buying several days' worth of cheese, but they didn't see the logic
in that, either. Eventually, I would give in and just hope that Murray
would not walk by at the exact moment that I was selling some
elderly gentleman an eighth of a pound of Vermont Cheddar. Back
then, I considered these customers an annoyance, but I realize
now that the ritual of shopping for their daily portion of cheese

was one way for these people to fill a calendar that didn't have all that much else in it.

All of the employees referred to Murray as Mr. Klein, except for members of the Zabar family. I was his favorite Zabar—most likely because I was smart, skilled at slicing cheese, and looked good behind the counter—and more often than not he was charming and complimentary to me. But there were also the baffling times when I experienced the full force of his wrath over such minor offenses as leaving stray pieces of Saran Wrap on the counter or being too slow to greet the customers. Then one Friday evening, after a particularly difficult day, my father mentioned that he and Murray had fought about something and weren't speaking to each other. Well, I thought to myself, that explained that.

Around this time, Gucci had opened an enormously popular new store on Fifth Avenue, and that year I saved up four paychecks—my take-home pay was sixteen dollars for an eight-hour day—so that I could buy a Gucci scarf. Some of the store's appeal lay in Gucci's haughty attitude toward their customers; they'd figured out that New Yorkers would go mad for a store where you practically had to beg the salesperson to show you the merchandise. I found this fascinating, because at Zabar's the customer was king, in addition to always being right. And so we were all surprised that Eli adopted the Gucci approach when, in July 1973, he opened E.A.T., his own gourmet food store on Madison Avenue between East Eightieth and Eighty-First Streets. It was a parallel gastronomic universe: instead of Zabar's low prices and cheerful air of chaos, E.A.T. was a hushed temple of highly expensive, curated fare. Designed by his then wife Abbie, it was also incredibly chic and spare. When he started out, Eli needed some experienced help behind the counter, so I worked for him as a salesperson the first week E.A.T. was open. It was summer and quiet on Madison Avenue when an older woman came in and asked for Jarlsberg cheese, which was a favorite among the customers at Zabar's. I searched the cheese counter thoroughly but couldn't find the Jarlsberg. When I asked Eli where it was, he said he didn't carry it. And when our disappointed customer asked why not, Eli glared at her and shouted, "Because it's a terrible cheese and I refuse to sell it!" Stunned, the woman scuttled out of the store. I doubted that she would ever return but did not discount the possibility that Eli's Gucci approach would work and she would ask for a more appropriate cheese the next time.

One thing Eli did retain was the Zabar passion for authenticity and quality. He still had wonderful memories of being a child in the store, taking in the delightful aromas of the pickles and sauerkraut, of the Eastern European Jewish countermen giving him tastes of smoked salmon and teaching him how to slice fish. He also believed the quality of food in New York City had diminished as the generation of immigrant bakers, butchers, greengrocers, chefs, and owners of ethnic specialty stores passed away. Eli had discovered another culinary world on his trips to Europe, and E.A.T. was inspired by the food halls and markets of London and Paris. It was his mission to revive American cuisine by sourcing and making the best food according to traditional production methods. Initially, he imported products from Europe and commissioned pâtés, breads, cheeses, salads, and jams from local merchants. Just like his father, Louis, and his brother Saul, he rejected any delivery that did not measure up to his exacting standards. But unlike Zabar's, E.A.T. offered the best quality at the *highest* price, because Eli put a great value on his effort and talent, and believed the customer should pay for it.

I never did tell Eli that, as the self-appointed culinary expert at Barnard, I had published some food-related articles in the *Columbia Daily Spectator,* including an educational tract entitled "Student Cheese," in which I extolled the virtues of Jarlsberg. During the early 1970s, imported cheeses had barely begun to gain popularity with the general public, and most of my fellow students were familiar only with sliced American, Swiss, Velveeta, and cream cheese. In another article I discussed yogurt, a newly trendy food, and compared several brands in great detail. My most in-depth review appeared as the cover story in a local publication called *Wisdom's Child,* for which I researched every aspect of fourteen Upper West Side movie theaters. Although I also opined on seating comfort, restrooms, and programming, my personal focus was on the refreshments—especially the popcorn. Only two theaters—the Riviera and the Edison—came up to my popcorn standards.

I was proud of my short career in culinary journalism, but Murray was truly unrivaled at getting the Zabar's name into the newspapers and magazines. His favorite publicity tool was a good price war. The first was the Cuisinart dispute. In 1973, Cuisinart introduced the food processor, which immediately became the hottest-selling food appliance in New York. But instead of selling it for the retail price of $190, Zabar's charged $135. The wholesale price was $120.

The quest to obtain a Cuisinart at the Zabar's low price became a test of urban mettle. Cynthia Van Allen Schaffner grew up in Iowa, married a New Yorker, and moved to the Upper East Side in 1972. At the time, Cynthia was working her way through *Mastering the Art of French Cooking* and was an avid watcher of *The French Chef.* As she told me when we became friends years later, "Around 1974, Julia Child became very excited about a new machine from France that chopped, kneaded, pureed, and julienned in seconds—a French Cuisinart! I had to have one. But they were expensive." Back in Iowa City, the only option was to buy an appliance like this at the retail price; if Cynthia couldn't afford it, she went without it. But New York City presented consumers with a wider range of purchasing options. When she saw an advertisement for Zabar's limited supply of Cuisinarts at 30 percent off, Cynthia saved up her shopping money, dipped into her savings, and got up early on the appointed day to stand in line to buy this wondrous machine. She admitted to feeling somewhat intimidated by the banter of the professional chefs who were waiting in line with her. "When the doors opened," Cynthia recalled, "the line became a throng, and against all my tendencies to demur, I elbowed my way through the crush. When I finally got close to the counter, I grabbed the clerk's arm, handed over my cash, and bought a brand-new French Cuisinart in its original box. By the time I got home, I was exhausted and triumphant. And that was the day my husband decided I'd become a New Yorker."

Not everyone was happy about the price-war excitement. Upset that Murray was undercharging for their product, in December 1975, Cuisinart informed Zabar's that it would not ship any more food processors to the store unless Zabar's sold them at the man-

ufacturer's suggested retail price. Viewing this threat as a challenge, Murray stopped buying directly from the manufacturer and
instead spent the next eight months hoarding Cuisinarts that he
was purchasing, in cash, from small retailers at prices above wholesale but below retail. When he had amassed 200 Cuisinarts, he
announced in *New York* magazine that he was once again selling
them at Zabar's at $135 apiece. Hundreds of people mobbed the
store. The food processors sold out immediately, and Murray gave
out rain checks for 966 more.

While Murray was buying up retail Cuisinarts wherever he could
find them, my father tackled the legal angle, with Zabar's suing
Cuisinart in federal court for restraint of trade. If Zabar's won,
the local Cuisinart distributor would have to supply the store with
food processors, regardless of the price Zabar's charged consumers for them. During the litigation process, the customers with
rain checks waited anxiously to see if they would be honored. The
case was finally settled out of court in December 1977, and Cuisinart provided Zabar's with enough food processors to honor the
rain checks; each one allowed its holder to purchase a Cuisinart
at the promised price of $135, which was at that point $5 *below*
the wholesale price. And with a triumphal flourish, Murray threw
in a free coffee grinder and five pounds of coffee with every food
processor. "It doesn't mean anything to me to lose a few thousand
dollars to make a point," he said in a newspaper interview. He'd
made no profit in the Cuisinart price war, but Murray had garnered
priceless publicity for the store.

The Cuisinart controversy was a sign of the changes the neighborhood began to undergo in the mid-1970s. The Upper West Side
was becoming a destination for gourmet retail stores and restaurants. In the fall of 1976, I was a graduate student in Columbia
University's Historic Preservation Program and still working in the
Zabar's cheese department. One day, a tall, handsome customer
who looked to be about fifteen years older than I purchased some
cheese and then asked me out to dinner at Ruskay's. Ruskay's was
a restaurant on Columbus Avenue that I'd heard much about but
that was way beyond my budget. Its expensive prix fixe menu
changed every day, and it was the first of a number of bistros in the

neighborhood that were created to reflect the distinctive culinary sensibilities of their up-and-coming chefs. The rough-and-tumble commercial storefronts of Columbus Avenue began to fill up with these restaurants, as well as with trendy clothing boutiques. Ruskay's long, narrow, high-ceilinged dining space could seat only twenty customers at a time. I wish I could remember what my date and I ate; all I remember is that it was delicious.

Nearby, Sheila Lukins and Julee Rosso opened The Silver Palate in 1977. They sold fresh, high-quality prepared foods and packaged goods that had been made according to their own simple but elegant recipes. This was take-out American fare on a higher level than had ever been available before. In 1982, Lukins and Rosso published the best-selling *Silver Palate Cookbook*. Home cooks following its recipes, including chicken Marbella with prunes, olives, and capers, would host dinner parties that were the height of 1980s chic.

A PARTICULARLY ARDUOUS TIME for Zabar's employees was the Thanksgiving to New Year's season. A jam-packed store full of customers who are always right would leave us all needing some sort of reward for making it through those eight pressure-filled weeks. It came in the form of the Zabar's annual employees' holiday party, which was held on a weekday evening after Christmas and attended by all the employees and their families, our food suppliers, and our accountants and lawyers. The store would close at 7:30, and a lavish buffet would be laid out on long tables in the aisles. There were cases of champagne and platters piled high with Scotch salmon, smoked whitefish, smoked turkey, hot roast beef, corned beef, and pâté de foie gras. This was all good and fine, but the real draw were the tables containing the only two items sold in the store that employees were not allowed to eat during their daily lunch breaks: beluga caviar and sturgeon.

In those days, the finest beluga came from Iran. The glistening black eggs tasted salty, sweet, and fresh. At the 1976 holiday party, David, Sandy, and my friend Adam Remez and I parked ourselves in front of the caviar station and ladled heaping spoons of beluga

David and me; my friend Adam Remez; and my sister, Sandy,
gorging ourselves at the 1976 Zabar's holiday party—one of the perks
of being a Zabar's employee and/or family member. (LARRY MORRIS/
THE NEW YORK TIMES/REDUX)

onto buttered bread. I've eaten more elaborate meals than this, but
I'm not sure I have ever eaten a better one standing up.

This was the party where Zabar's employee George Bordansky
celebrated his sixty-fifth birthday and his retirement after thirty-
five years at the store. Georgie was a short, gruff appetizing man
with a formidable white mustache. From the perspective of my
twenty-two-year-old self, Georgie seemed ancient. He'd begun
working for my grandfather in 1941, and after retiring he went
from slicing fish behind the counter to becoming a salmon consultant to Saul. His job was to arrive at the smokehouses before
Saul did, to evaluate and select smoked salmon for Saul's approval.
He knew Saul liked the salmon lean, with just a little bit of fat.
Among the cognoscenti, Georgie was considered the best picker
of smoked salmon in the world.

The employee parties were for the workers, not for the rich
and famous, but that year we had a celebrity Upper West Sider as
a guest—the author Joseph Heller. He was there because his best

friend, Irving "Speed" Vogel, was a painter and sculptor who was employed by my uncle as a herring taster at Zabar's. Heller was a regular customer and lived with his family in the Apthorp, a block away from the store. Heller often crossed paths with Saul at the YMCA on West Sixty-Third Street, just off Central Park West, where he and Vogel worked out along with a circle that included Israel Horovitz, Paddy Chayefsky, and Paul Simon. In a feature for *The New York Times Magazine,* Barbara Gelb wrote about Heller's "basically unglamorous Gang of Four" of "same old friends," which included Vogel and sometimes expanded to include Mario Puzo and Mel Brooks, and she described Speed as "a retired textile manufacturer and a former itinerant herring taster for Zabar's." Years later, in *No Laughing Matter,* a book he cowrote with Heller, Vogel retorted that he could accept the characterizations of "same old friends," but "since when by them is an itinerant herring taster for Zabar's not glamorous?"

"We did not worship at a synagogue or church," Joseph Heller's daughter, Erica, wrote to me years later. "Our holy place was—and is—Zabar's. Every Sunday morning my dad and I would make the slow trek (actually 123 steps from Zabar's to the Apthorp) as if from our shtetl, dragging back bags and bags of bagels, onions, cream cheese, kippered salmon, sable, tomatoes, pickles, and, finally, rugelach. With the Sunday *New York Times* spread out over my parents' bed doing double duty as a tablecloth, we'd chatter and chew away, until what had looked like enough food for fifty starving truck drivers was reduced to a few pitiful crumbs on a platter. This was our weekly ritual. Regardless of moodiness, lack of sleep, having been out too late the night before, or with hours of dreaded homework stretching out before us, the four of us came together this way every Sunday, and it always ended up with laughter.

"My father loved his life—writing books and acting the role of celebrity. But one day, I took a walk in Riverside Park with the two of them, and Dad was definitely sulking as Speed kept dipping his hand into a Zabar's bag of tasty olives. Finally, my father brayed, like a four-year-old, 'How come YOU get to be at Zabar's all day eating, and I have to go write books?' Speed stopped walking and considered his response thoughtfully. 'You have to write books so that Philip Roth doesn't win the Nobel (he didn't), and I have to work at Zabar's because I'm having too much fun and will surely be fired soon.' (He was.)"

By 1976, Murray had transformed Zabar's into a $6 million gourmet emporium featuring food and houseware items from all over the world. Following in Louis Zabar's footsteps, he was on a never-ending hunt for products of the best quality to be sold at the best price. There was only one problem: Zabar's was now bursting at the seams.

Fortunately, my father's true passion is for real estate. He spent seven years wooing their landlord and, finally, in 1978, Saul, Stanley, and Murray bought the Zabar's building and the four other contiguous properties along Broadway between Eightieth and Eighty-First Streets, including the northernmost building, where Zabar's began in 1934. The partners leased the storefront in the corner building on Eightieth Street to Delices La Cote Basque, a French pastry shop that also served Zabar's coffee, and they took over the storefront between the pastry shop and Zabar's, which had been occupied by Beck's Drugstore. All this new space allowed Murray to indulge his love of kitchen appliances and housewares to such an extent that they grew to account for 10 to 12 percent of Zabar's sales.

As Zabar's was beginning to expand, New York City was starting to recover from the hard economic times that had almost bankrupted the city, which had stemmed in part from the national recession of 1973–75 and which had hit New York especially hard. With financial help from President Gerald Ford's federal government not an option (famously occasioning, in 1975, the New York *Daily News*'s front-page headline "Ford to City: Drop Dead"), Governor Hugh Carey created the Municipal Assistance Corporation, headed by Felix Rohatyn, which advanced funds to New York City and guided it to fiscal health.

During those difficult years, the Upper West Side was dubbed the "Wild West" by some residents of other New York City neighborhoods. Because of budget cuts at the sanitation department, the sidewalks and streets were scattered with litter. The peeling benches on the pedestrian islands that separated Broadway's uptown and downtown traffic were filled with drunks sipping from bottles in paper bags, junkies shaking and muttering to themselves, prostitutes in hot pants taking a break between customers, and indomitable elderly women who just wanted to get a bit of sun. I don't know how those ladies did it. I myself was more than a little apprehensive when I crossed those islands, and the whistles and catcalls of the ever-present construction workers on the streets only added to the unpleasantness of going to school and to work. Zabar's had its share of distressing encounters, too. A homeless woman who stalked the streets in house slippers and carrying a shopping bag would routinely wander into the store screaming, "Bastards, all of you!" When I left the house every morning, I made sure I had enough cash in case I was mugged, and I was careful to watch that no one was following me into the subway.

But even though some left the neighborhood, many of Zabar's middle- and upper-middle-class customers remained on the Upper West Side, and we acquired new customers from among the young professionals who were moving into the neighborhood and the empty nesters who were returning from the suburbs. Despite—or, more accurately, because of—the heartbreaking urban blight, it was a buyer's market for real estate throughout Manhattan, particularly on the Upper West Side. When my parents moved back to Manhattan from Queens in 1973, they could have bought a ten-room apartment in The Beresford on Central Park West for thirty thousand dollars (alas, my mother felt that the rooms didn't get enough sun). While I was attending law school from 1977 to 1980, I rented a four-room apartment on Eighty-Fourth Street, facing Riverside Park, for four hundred dollars a month. Artists, actors, dancers, musicians, singers, writers, and professors had no trouble finding reasonably priced places to live, and back then the theater, ballet, opera, and museums were affordable even to people with limited incomes. As the city slowly recovered, jobs were plentiful, and new shops opened along Broadway and Columbus Avenue. The future seemed bright.

Zabar's pursuit of more space was not without controversy. The upper floors of the four-building complex that Saul, Stanley, and Murray had just bought were occupied by a single-room-occupancy hotel called The Centre. Its entrance was on Eightieth Street, just around the corner from Zabar's entrance. The hotel's manager had long been criticized by the community for housing in substandard apartments prostitutes, drug addicts, alcoholics, and patients who had been recently released from mental hospitals and were sometimes violent and disruptive. This was not something Saul, Stanley, and Murray wanted any part of, and they knew they could use the space for offices and storage. Zabar's initiated eviction proceedings against the manager of the hotel, the DWL Hotel Corporation, for nonpayment of rent. Zabar's also claimed that some of the tenants threw objects out of the windows of their rooms, including garbage and, one time, a typewriter, jeopardizing the safety of customers and pedestrians. Some of the residents accused Zabar's of harassment; they claimed services in the hotel had been suspended after the eviction proceedings commenced, but the head of the Mayor's Office of Single Room Occupancy Housing admitted that it was the DWL management company that had abandoned the hotel six months before the eviction. The Centre was one of seven residential hotels on the Upper West Side where tenants faced possible eviction during that winter of 1979. It was a difficult time. I remember seeing tenants, politicians, and neighborhood supporters picketing in front of the store. On December 29, with demonstrators chanting "People before fish!" and carrying placards reading ZABAR'S—ILLEGAL, IMMORAL, FATTENING, my father came out of the store, stood before the group of about fifty protesters, and promised to restore essential services and not to evict the remaining tenants for three months—or as long as it took to relocate the tenants—as soon as Zabar's took legal possession of the hotel from DWL. He also agreed to meet with the representatives of the hotel's newly organized tenants' association. By 1981, the hotel's tenants and Zabar's had come to a $200,000 relocation settlement.

With the hotel emptied, Zabar's was poised for a major renovation of the second and third floors. The primary reason for the expansion was the creation of an additional ten thousand square feet of selling space for housewares on the second floor, which Murray named The Mezzanine. (In 1982, the store would also take over the northernmost storefront, which had been a dry-cleaning business.) Moreover, there was new office space for Grandma Lilly's cousins Pearl and Joy Watman, the mother and daughter team who managed Zabar's finances. Until then, their paper-filled office was a tiny room above the Zabar's kitchen, where they prepared a weekly payroll for 110 employees and paid every bill received within a week. Murray's respectful treatment of his suppliers was part of his overall business strategy. "If we get a bill on Monday, we pay it on Friday," he would say, "because then we get a better price and are treated better. And, of course, when there's some [product that's] new or special, they come to us [first]." Zabar's employs this payment schedule to this day.

The third Watman in the Zabar's office was Pearl's younger daughter, Andrea. Talented, beloved, and with a great sense of humor, Andrea wore many hats at Zabar's for more than thirty years as the store's creative director and as head of customer service, catering, graphic design, and the mail-order catalog, until her untimely death in 2011.

Once The Mezzanine was up and running, Murray proceeded to stock up on housewares and hardware. He went to Europe several times a year to seek out new products, always paying in cash so that he could in turn offer food processors, mixers, pots, coffee makers, and coffee grinders at the lowest prices in New York. One time, Murray went to France and came home with forty-eight duck presses. Although at $250 each the duck presses were expensive, Murray claimed that another New York store was charging $400 each for them, and he wasn't worried about finding forty-eight customers for such an esoteric appliance. He was right, of course. Zabar's also became the largest importer of copper pots in the country. And the store sold more espresso makers in one year— some costing as much as $1,000—than any other New York City retailer. That was in addition to the thousands of food processors and coffee grinders sold each year.

Murray's quest for new products wasn't limited to housewares. One day, he decided to rent an in-house croissant-baking oven instead of continuing to purchase croissants from a bakery in Brooklyn. Every twenty minutes, a voice on the loudspeaker announced the availability of a freshly baked batch—resulting in the sale of twenty-three thousand croissants per week. The success of in-store croissant production inspired Murray to also purchase a cookie-baking oven. This he strategically placed in the front of the store. The delicious aroma of freshly baked cookies was irresistible, and customers purchased two thousand pounds of cookies each week.

Another ingredient in the store's success was the relationships Saul, Stanley, and Murray developed with the Zabar's staff. Murray ran a tight operation, to the point where he would advise employees not to call in sick "unless they were dead" (which the staff understood to be only a bit of an exaggeration on his part). But he was fair as well, and he and my father and my uncle encouraged their employees to feel that they played a major part in maintaining and developing the personality of the business. Zabar's does demand dedication and loyalty from its staff, but it's known throughout the industry that the store compensates its personnel at a rate higher than similar businesses. Qualified employees participate in a profit-sharing plan and a bonus program. All three partners knew that both policies are great incentives for increased worker productivity. Employees are expected to be knowledgeable about the products for which they are responsible and to treat all customers—celebrity and otherwise—with courtesy and respect. And the store provides financial assistance for employees who are going through difficult times. There are always opportunities for talented and hardworking staff to advance; some employees started as cashiers and eventually became managers. A valuable by-product of these policies is that Zabar's is able to avoid costly worker turnover.

For some long-term employees, working at Zabar's became the center of their lives. And for at least one staff member, it became the center of his afterlife as well. When quintessential deli man Howard Sommers died in 2011, his family requested that his ashes be mixed in the soil of a potted plant onto which a brass memorial plaque had been affixed. It was Howard's dying wish that his remains reside at Zabar's; the potted plant now lives on a windowsill facing Broadway in the second-floor conference room, where the office staff carefully tends to it to this day.

As the 1980s progressed, Zabar's kept growing. By 1981, annual gross sales were about $15 million—which is to say, $4,500 per square foot of selling space. This was the highest sales-to-space volume of any food store in America. But as Zabar's prospered, my part-time employment at the store came to an end. Although I loved eating, my work there did not inspire me to enter the culinary world. I just wasn't interested in preparing, selling, or serving food and felt my talents lay elsewhere. I also knew from the inside the emotional stress and challenges involved in running a family business, and I wanted to avoid them. Fortunately, other third-generation Zabars did not feel the same way. I had received an MS in historic preservation at Columbia University, a JD from NYU School of Law, and I had been a real estate associate at a law firm for two years before leaving in 1982 to become the first director of the New York City Historic Properties Fund, a revolving loan fund for historic-property owners that was part of the New York Landmarks Conservancy. That year, I also married Mark Mariscal, an architect originally from Phoenix who had come to New York after graduating from Rice University and fell in love with the city, Jewish culture, pastrami and corned beef, and, most especially, me. Mark wasn't Jewish when we met, but he eventually took conversion classes at our Reform synagogue, Congregation Rodeph Sholom, and fate led him to a career designing yeshivas and synagogues in the tristate area.

When I introduced Mark to Grandma Lilly, I was honest about his not being Jewish. I was rather shocked when she asked me later if he was circumcised, but without missing a beat, I simply replied, "How should I know?" To my vast relief, that seemed to work. I was happy to see that Grandma Lilly liked Mark even though he wasn't Jewish. Because he was tall and slender, with dark hair and big blue eyes, she always referred to him as "your Handsome Husband" instead of by his name.

I was now watching what was going on at the store from afar, but there was no escaping the publicity Murray continued to generate for Zabar's. Rather than focusing on traditional advertising, he sought to increase sales by creating controversy. As the Cuisinart battle was past history, Murray moved on to instigating skirmishes with The Cellar, Macy's popular food and housewares department.

He started with, of all things, a Lindt chocolate bar. Both stores had been selling the bar at $1.39, but then Zabar's lowered their price first to 98 cents and then to 89 cents. Macy's countered with 39 cents, and Zabar's responded by cutting their price to 35 cents, which was where this particular war ended.

Other small battles followed, but these were just practice maneuvers. One time, Murray filled the windows at Zabar's with pages from the Macy's housewares catalog and undercut every price by 30 percent. Another time he placed a three- by four-foot placard in the Zabar's window, with WHAT DOES MACY'S KNOW ABOUT CHEESE? in bold lettering at the top and HOW TO CHARGE EXORBITANT PRICES! right below it. Underneath was a chart comparing Zabar's and Macy's cheese prices. The Zabar's prices were, of course, dramatically lower.

There was more. Several months before the 1983 holiday season, when caviar was selling for $180.00 to $200.00 per fourteen-ounce tin, Zabar's cut its price to $149.95. Although Macy's usually held its caviar sale between Christmas and New Year's, this time Macy's responded by reducing its price of malassol caviar to $145.00 just before Thanksgiving. Then, a week before Christmas, they went down to $139.95. Murray countered with $129.95 and Macy's shot back with $125.00. Murray made the last reduction, to $119.95. "They are trying to bring me to my knees," Murray told *The New York Times,* "but they won't." When he warned, "Blood will run in the streets," we knew he meant business in Murray-speak. By contrast, Macy's denied there even was a war. A spokesperson for Macy's stated, "We are not, repeat not, in a war. We are doing business. We never comment on anybody else's business and we hope they would not comment on ours."

The Great Caviar War was a clever publicity stunt, positioning Zabar's as a scrappy David to Macy's corporate Goliath. It attracted more attention than any advertising campaign could have provided. Even *The New York Times* discussed Zabar's "Battle of Beluga on Manhattan's West Side" in a tongue-in-cheek editorial about gourmet food conflicts entitled "Where the Next War Will Start."

The Cuisinart and caviar wars illustrated Murray's love for the "loss leader" strategy in sales. He lured the customers into the store

Sam Cohen and Kenny Sze look on as Murray proffers a heaping tin of caviar while he plots his next move in the Great Caviar War, circa 1983. Sam was a lox cutter extraordinaire; Kenny, also an appetizing man, went on to found Sable's on the Upper East Side with his brother. (COPYRIGHT © ZABAR'S AND COMPANY, INC. ALL RIGHTS RESERVED.)

with a fabulous bargain, knowing that once they were inside, they could be enticed into buying any number of other items. Any loss he took on the bait would be made up on other purchases. Murray was also the master of another selling technique called twisting, which means constantly rearranging the merchandise to make customers think they are seeing something new.

For the thirty thousand customers who came into the store each week, the biggest sellers were the basics. Fish: five thousand pounds each week, including two thousand pounds of smoked salmon and fifteen hundred pounds of pickled herring. Cheese: two thousand pounds each week of Brie alone. Meat: three thousand pounds of smoked meat per week. And, of course, coffee: eight thousand pounds a week. During Murray's tenure, Zabar's sold its smoked salmon at cost, because marking it up would make it too expensive for the customers. Saul, who was in charge of the fish department, was in total agreement with this policy. Moreover, he refused to sell any smoked fish he had not personally tasted and selected on his trips each week to the smokehouses in Brooklyn. He was willing to pay top dollar for the freshest fish available, even when he knew the store would not make a profit on it.

Saul also paid the highest prices for the best coffee beans. Displayed in overflowing barrels, the beans were ground to the customer's specifications and then packed in expensive coated bags to maintain the coffee's freshness. Zabar's coffee is another product that was priced much lower than coffee sold anywhere else. For any item sold in the store, if the best or freshest wasn't available at a particular time, or if the price the wholesaler was asking was deemed to be too high, Zabar's would not stock the item until it met Saul, Stanley, and Murray's criteria for quality and cost.

The ongoing drama and gourmet offerings at Zabar's attracted plenty of celebrities, but the store made a point of treating all of its customers equally. This was all well and good until the celebrities discovered that Zabar's did *not* deliver. Ever. Many famous people were taken aback at being expected to schlep their own groceries home. According to Fred Ferretti, who wrote an article about Zabar's for *New York* magazine in 1982, Leonard Bernstein wanted a delivery of smoked whitefish to his apartment in The Dakota and when Zabar's said no, he swore he would never shop at the store again. He did come back, eventually—or, more accurately, he would send the housekeeper he shared with Lauren Bacall (another Zabar's customer) to the store to pick up his order. In recognition of Bernstein's return, Zabar's granted him one of their extremely rare charge accounts. Joy Watman always said these charge accounts were "better than Tiffany's."

Rules are, of course, made to be broken, and it was Joy who decided which customers were exempt from the no-delivery rule. Barbra Streisand was a notable example. Joy was a big fan, and when Streisand was in New York, Joy would personally deliver her order. "Barbra likes herring and sturgeon," she told Ferretti, "and she can get *any* special treatment here. Anything."

Another exception, Pearl Watman conceded, was for Bob Hope: "Hope was at the Waldorf Towers and he needed decaffeinated coffee, *our* decaffeinated, on an emergency basis," she told Ferretti. "So we delivered it. But it was an *emergency*. Be sure to say it was an emergency."

Joy also admitted to Ferretti, somewhat reluctantly, that Zabar's delivered to Lutèce. "Lutèce buys all its smoked salmon from us. You really can't expect Mr. Soltner [the owner/chef of the legendary restaurant, which closed in 2004] to pick up. He's so busy. So, we deliver. But only there. *Nobody* else. Be sure to say nobody else."

Other famous customers (to whom Zabar's did not deliver) included Eli Wallach, Morley Safer, Lucie Arnaz, Alan King, Adolph Green, Pia Lindström, Warner LeRoy, Andy Warhol, Judy Collins, Roger Grimsby, Neil Sedaka, Joan Rivers, Calvin Klein, Tony Roberts, Beverly Sills, and Mel Brooks. According to Ferretti, Zabar's provided Eli Wallach's New Year's Day turkey, William Paley's smoked brook trout, Faye Dunaway's chicken salad, and Gilda Radner's many varieties of smoked fish. Zabar's also shipped packages to Jerry Lewis, wherever he happened to be in the United States. His usual order was two pounds of nova lox, one filleted whitefish, two packages of Philadelphia cream cheese, six lemons, six tomatoes, and two dozen bagels, lightly baked.

In the 1980s, the store instituted a no-personal-service rule and stopped filling phone orders. Customers had to come to the store in person to shop, unless they were placing a catering order. Of course, there was an exception to that, too—but only for Adnan Khashoggi, the Saudi businessman. When Khashoggi's yacht was in and he was staying at his apartment in Olympic Tower, Murray would turn the store inside out for him. Khashoggi's steward would order thousands of dollars of food, including many tins of caviar. And when items that Zabar's didn't stock appeared on the shopping list, Murray scurried to butchers and wine stores to get the complete order filled within twenty-four hours. For this personal attention, Murray charged a healthy "assembling fee," which Khashoggi happily paid.

Magazine and newspaper articles about the price wars and the celebrity customers helped spread the word about Zabar's way beyond the greater New York area. What also helped was that the store was beginning to appear in books, in movies, and on television shows. One of the earliest mentions was in Saul Bellow's 1970 novel *Mr. Sammler's Planet,* in which Artur Sammler, a Holocaust survivor living on the Upper West Side, kept a supply of onion rolls from Zabar's in his room. In 1979, Neil Simon filmed a scene from *Chapter Two* in the store, with James Caan and Marsha Mason shopping in the aisles. Zabar's was close to Simon's heart. He once wrote, "When I die and go to heaven, I hope the Zabar's up there is as good as the one down here."

Woody Allen mentioned Zabar's in a short story called "The Lunatic's Tale" that appeared in *The New Republic* in 1977. In it, he describes a woman with "skin like satin, or should I say like the finest of Zabar's novy." And he filmed a scene from his 1979 movie *Manhattan* in Zabar's. The shoot lasted for hours, beginning at night after the store closed and ending early in the morning. Almost all of it wound up on the cutting-room floor except for a memorable minute or so of Allen and Diane Keaton outside the store, staring longingly into the Zabar's display windows. But that was enough for the arbiters of pop culture. As recently as 2017, Zabar's appeared in a *New York Times* crossword puzzle as the answer to "Famed deli seen in Woody Allen's *Manhattan.*"

But it was not all smooth sailing. In 1982, the fully expanded Zabar's faced a new rival in the neighborhood: DDL Foodshow. Until then, for about a half century, Zabar's had competed amicably for the smoked fish clientele with Barney Greengrass on Amsterdam Avenue and Murray's Sturgeon Shop slightly to the north on Broadway. Fairway, founded in 1933, focused on fruits and vegetables, and Citarella, established in 1912, was known for their fresh fish and meat. But now that gourmet food was chic and glamorous, Fairway and Citarella expanded their wares to compete for serious foodie customers, and a newly energized Columbus Avenue began to sprout restaurants, food shops, and boutiques. In late November 1982, the movie producer Dino De Laurentis opened his lavish DDL Foodshow at Eighty-First and Columbus Avenue. Unlike the homey décor of Zabar's, Barney Greengrass, and Murray's, DDL was a movie set of a delicatessen designed by the noted interior designer Adam Tihany: it was lavishly tiled and boasted wide brick arches, polished wood, and gleaming brass, all highlighted with theatrical lighting. Bryan Miller, then the food critic for *The New York Times,* wrote, "DDL is as similar to Barney Greengrass as the Chrysler Building is to a phone booth." Another difference was DDL's ethnic identity. Unlike the Jewish Upper West Side triumvirate, DDL offered Italian specialties. The first weekend it attracted more than thirty thousand customers, but the owners of the old-guard shops said they weren't worried. Murray Klein predicted that a lot of people were going to look at the showplace and then come back to Zabar's. In an interview with Gael Greene, Murray claimed De Laurentis had even tried to hire him. "On a Saturday he came to Zabar's. I should take time to talk on a Saturday? . . . I said, 'Buy Zabar's and you can have me.'" Murray always said DDL wouldn't last, and several months after it opened, *New York Times* food critic Mimi Sheraton reviewed the prepared and unprepared offerings and was not impressed by the food or the service. Unlike the knowledgeable and experienced salesmen at the established stores who enjoyed kibitzing with the customers, the young salespeople at DDL knew little about what they were selling.

In the meantime, the culinary revolution was spreading beyond the Upper West Side and extending throughout the city. In addition to DDL, other retail contenders included Glorious Food, Pasta and Cheese, Dean & DeLuca, and Balducci's. Eli continued to operate E.A.T. on Madison and Eighty-First Street, his businesses thriving in spite of his brusque retail manner. The main E.A.T. store was now located on the ground floor of the Rhinelander Mansion on Madison and Seventy-Second Street (it's currently the Ralph Lauren men's store). This store, also designed by Abbie, was beautiful in its European austerity, with a black-and-white marble checkerboard floor and mezzanine office guarded by a classical stone balustrade. Eli also maintained a small satellite at Henri Bendel, an iconic, cutting-edge women's apparel and accessories store that closed in 2019 after 123 years in business.

Murray was right about DDL, which closed two years after it opened. But it did leave its mark. When Eataly debuted in 2010, Sam Sifton, then the food critic for *The New York Times,* saw DDL and Dean & DeLuca in SoHo as early prototypes of the vast Italian food emporium. DDL was beautiful, but customers came back to Zabar's shlumpy, haphazard interior because they felt like part of the Zabar family—or at least imagined that they were. Nora Ephron articulated this relationship with the store in the 1984 *New York Times* article that spurred my mother to invite her to brunch. Ephron was fond of Russ & Daughters on the Lower East Side and of Murray's Sturgeon Shop, but she was obsessed with Zabar's. Ephron lived a block away from the store in the Apthorp, where Joseph Heller had also lived, and she would come by five or six times a week.

"Sometimes I imagine I am a Zabar," she wrote. "I imagine that we Zabars all live together in a West Side apartment with pots and pans hanging from the living-room ceiling. I imagine that every night those of us who have worked at the store that day bring home six kinds of bread and the week's smoked salmon special and the latest Italian cheese and the Virginia peanuts. I imagine that we sit around blindfolded conducting taste tests on the relative merits of, say, the beluga and the sevruga, and I imagine we have bitter fights about how to eliminate the congestion at the cash registers and how to get the space in which we plan to expand to look as cluttered and discombobulated as the rest of the store. In my mind's eye, on the outskirts of all this, Zabar children scamper around, nibbling chocolate croissants."

Ephron wrote that at first she thought she created this fantasy because she wanted to be a princess in a Jewish royal family. "But the truth is I like to imagine I am a Zabar because I think of myself as family, and since Zabar's doesn't treat me as family, I have to do it unilaterally."

When I read Ephron's article, what struck me was how accurately she imagined our family. There were a few exceptions—the pots and pans hung in the kitchen, not in the living room, and all the Zabars did not live together. But my father continued to bring home food for taste testing and discussion (though without the benefit of blindfolds), and at family holidays the children did run around the table in circles while the adults talked. At home we did not have bitter fights about how to eliminate congestion at the cash registers—although Saul, Stanley, and Murray probably did in the store—but we did discuss possible solutions to other logistical problems over dinner.

Ephron was right that sometimes the conversation was not relaxed. Saul brought his same rigorous culinary standards to family gatherings, criticizing the food while he ate. One Rosh Hashanah at my parents' apartment, Saul called my mother's brisket inedible so many times that my mother finally responded, "Saul, if it's inedible, why did you finish everything on your plate?" I'd like to say that Saul is an exception, but his comments were evidence of another trait inherited by several members of my family: no filter.

Although Murray wasn't a Zabar, he had no filter, either. This trait may have been responsible for the frequent clashes among Murray, Saul, and Stanley when their spheres of responsibility overlapped. For a long time, those fights were just how the store worked. But as Murray's unhappiness increased, it became evident these conflicts were no longer business as usual.

Lilly Zabar's Stuffed Cabbage

Adapted by Judith Zabar
Edited and tested by Monita Buchwald

This is my favorite of Grandma Lilly's recipes. When my mother makes her adapted recipe, I love the combination of sweet and savory flavors. Stuffed cabbage tastes best if it's made the day before, to allow it to absorb all that good sauce. This recipe can be doubled, with cabbage rolls frozen for another time.

MAKES ABOUT 24 STUFFED CABBAGES; SERVES 8 TO 10

INGREDIENTS

1 large head green cabbage (about 4 pounds)
½ cup apricot preserves
One 15-ounce can stewed tomatoes
1½ cups water
Juice of 1 lemon
¼ cup packed dark or light brown sugar
½ cup raisins or currants

2 garlic cloves, minced
2 pounds ground beef
½ cup uncooked white rice
1½ teaspoons kosher salt
¼ teaspoon freshly ground black pepper
1 large egg
1 medium onion, grated
¼ cup ketchup
Tomato juice or stock if needed

DIRECTIONS

1. Core the cabbage and place it in a large pot with water to cover. Bring to a boil and then simmer, covered, for about 10 minutes, until wilted. Drain; cover with cold water and drain again. (Alternatively, you can place the cored cabbage in the freezer for a few

days. Defrost 24 hours before making the stuffed cabbage. It will wilt naturally.)

2. Combine the preserves, tomatoes, 1 cup of the water, the lemon juice, and brown sugar in a saucepan. Bring to a boil. Add the raisins and garlic and stir until combined. Remove from the heat and cover.

3. Combine the beef, rice, salt, pepper, egg, onion, the remaining ½ cup water, and the ketchup in a large bowl. Blend with your fingers until well mixed.

4. Pull off the tough outer leaves of the cabbage and discard. Remove the big veins with a V cut in the other leaves, if necessary. Chop any leftover cabbage and reserve it to put on top of the cabbage rolls in the pot. Any leftover filling can be made into meatballs.

5. Pull off the inside leaves and place them one by one on a flat surface, outside down. Fill with 2 or 3 heaping tablespoons of filling, depending on the leaf size. Fold up like an envelope: top first, then bottom, then the two sides. Place, seam side down, in one layer in a large Dutch oven. You can add a few more on top.

6. Pour the sauce over the stuffed cabbage and simmer, covered, for 2 hours.

7. Preheat the oven to 300°F.

8. Place the stuffed cabbage in the oven and cook, uncovered, for another 30 minutes, or until heated through. Add tomato juice or stock if more liquid is needed.

9

Trouble in Gourmet Paradise,
1985–95

AS WE RANG IN 1985, A THRIVING ZABAR'S WAS ATTRACTING ONE MIL-lion customers per year. Its five adjacent storefronts comprised 12,500 square feet of selling space, and sales per square foot were still the highest of any store in America. Annual sales were between $20 million and $25 million. Net profit was close to $4 million. A famous gourmet institution of long-standing in New York, Zabar's was now a national gastronomic icon as well.

But despite all this success, Saul, Stanley, and Murray were not getting along. Unless they had to meet to discuss a particular busi-ness issue, they did not speak to one another at the store. Each partner handled his own area of responsibility as if he were in a silo. Grandma Lilly, no longer an owner and totally uninvolved in the business, was not in a position to act as peacemaker. She was spending most of her time in Miami Beach or Mohegan. Lilly was a widow for the second time; Louis Chartoff had died in 1978. All the Zabars continued to gather for holidays, weddings, and bar/bat mitzvahs, and they and the Kleins attended one another's family celebrations, but there was a chill in the air at these events, and social relationships among the couples were strained.

The main source of contention was that Murray, who was sixty-two years old, wanted to retire. He said he wanted a few years to learn how to enjoy life before he died. He begged my uncle and my father—who were, respectively, fifty-six and fifty-two—to buy him out. They declined. Saul and Stanley did not want Murray to retire. Neither of them wanted to take over Murray's daunt-ing responsibility of the day-to-day management of the store, but most of all they understood that Murray's marketing savvy was

*Zabar's in 1985, after Saul, Stanley, and Murray acquired and
expanded the store into five contiguous buildings.* (COPYRIGHT
© ZABAR'S AND COMPANY, INC. ALL RIGHTS RESERVED.)

the reason behind the financial success of Zabar's. Strictly based
on their stockholders' agreement, Saul and Stanley's position was
justified. The agreement did not allow for retirement; the only way
a partner could leave was if he became totally disabled or died.
This unusual clause was a 1983 amendment to their original 1965
agreement, which all three partners had agreed to at the time. (It's
quite possible that Stanley and Saul were already anticipating Murray's imminent burnout.) In any case, it seemed as though the only
way to get past this impasse was to sell the store. One *Daily News*
reporter, Jonathan Mandell, dubbed the situation a real-life Jewish
version of the hit television series *Dynasty*.

In January 1985, the partners hired the brokerage firm Bear
Stearns to look into finding a buyer. The Zabar's customers were,
of course, shocked to hear that their beloved store might be on

the market. "The entire West Side is having a nervous breakdown over this," wrote a bereft Nora Ephron in *The New York Times*. One day in March, a whole line of customers at the cash-only register noticed Saul nearby and yelled in unison, "Don't sell!"

Murray was the most enthusiastic of the partners about the sale, telling anyone who would listen that he had to leave Zabar's before he was carried out. My uncle and my father were far more uncertain about the prospect of leaving Zabar's behind. Their personal and professional identities were entwined and embedded within the store. But they were also tired of the stresses of the partnership and wanted to ensure the longevity of Zabar's as an institution.

Shortly after word got out, David Liederman, the owner of the David's Cookies chain, put together a group of investors and approached Zabar's with an offer to buy the store. Liederman regarded Murray as his mentor in the food world, and as part of his offer, he asked Murray to stay on for at least two years during the transition. Liederman intended to open a number of Zabar's outlets in the United States, Europe, and Japan. To the press, he promised that he would do nothing to change the store's fundamental character, acknowledging that the clutter, noise, and jostling crowds were key to the Zabar's experience. Nevertheless, customers feared Liederman would turn Zabar's into a soulless chain of franchises.

Murray, Saul, and Stanley refused to comment to the press about the sale and the rumors of this and other offers. But Murray and Saul were quite willing to discuss their love-hate relationship. (My father refused to comment to the press entirely.) Saul admitted that although he and Murray did not speak to each other unless it was business, they had a very strong bond. Murray seemed to share Saul's ambivalence. He quipped to Jonathan Mandell, "We talk when we have something to talk about. We just haven't had something to talk about for years." But then, smiling, he likened his relationship with Saul to that of a brother. "Even now, I would give my life for either of them," he said in several interviews. "I'd go in a fire to pull them out."

In actual fact, Murray's attitude toward my father was more fraught. "I think it would take a team of psychologists many years to figure out the relationship between Murray and Stanley," David

Liederman told Mandell. But my mother and I did eventually figure it out: Murray's mercurial personality, risk-taking entrepreneurial skills, and over-the-top ambition were very much like my grandfather Louis's. Stanley reacted to Murray as a son would to a difficult father figure. Sometimes they praised each other extravagantly, and other times they were so furious with each other that they could not speak at all. There were times when my father's relationships with Murray and Saul became so tense that he would have to absent himself from the store for a while.

It was now September, and nothing had been resolved. David Liederman's first bid had not succeeded for lack of financing, but he continued trying to raise the funds to meet the price of $30 million for the business and the property that was being bandied about. Other bidders had also emerged, including a group of private investors in association with a major financial institution led by Michael Kapon, the owner of Acker, Merrall & Condit, a legendary wineshop on Broadway between Eighty-Sixth and Eighty-Seventh Streets. Kapon was particularly interested in the real estate portion of the purchase because his store was in a building about to be demolished. It appeared that he intended to continue to operate Zabar's and to locate his liquor business in a separate section of the building, as required by New York State law.

But then David Liederman returned with sufficient financing, and it looked as if the sale might finally go through. He offered $26.5 million, to be financed by junk bonds issued by Drexel Burnham Lambert. There seemed to be a deal, but when the parties met for the closing, the whole thing fell apart in the last fifteen minutes. In his 1992 *New York* magazine article "The War at Zabar's," Peter Hellman referenced David Liederman's account of the meeting, in which Liederman claimed that a nearly $30 million deal dissolved because the parties couldn't agree on Saul, Stanley, and Murray's future discount on Zabar's products.

This minor point of contention was, of course, just an excuse. In fact, Saul and Stanley did not truly want to sell, and by now even Murray was ambivalent; he felt guilty about abandoning his employees. And none of them was interested enough in the money to go through with the deal. They all lived in nice but not luxurious

Upper West Side apartments near the store, and neither they nor their wives cared about fancy cars or designer clothes or country homes. Saul rode a secondhand bike to work and his wardrobe consisted of worn khakis, a polo shirt, and a frayed Zabar's sweatshirt that he refused to throw out. My father's and Murray's work clothes were several notches above Saul's, but still far from high style. Their weekend houses were in Fire Island and Mohegan Colony, not the Hamptons. David Liederman was hugely disappointed that a deal that took a year to put together was derailed in fifteen minutes, but he understood what was truly distressing Saul, Stanley, and Murray.

In the long run, it was for the best that the sale didn't go through. Almost every gourmet food enterprise that went public or was sold to a corporate entity over the past thirty years is now either in financial trouble or no longer exists. David's Cookies, Balducci's, Dean & DeLuca, and Fairway are all shadows of their former selves. The lesson for our family was simple: no matter what a prospective purchaser promises, a corporation will be either unable or unwilling to maintain the eccentric soul that is the heart of Zabar's and its ongoing success.

But that left the partners right back where they'd started. Murray was still demanding his freedom; what he really wanted was for Saul and Stanley to buy him out. And they continued to refuse to do so. So from 1985 on, Murray coped by doing less. He made a serious attempt to stop coming in at 6:00 a.m. to open the store. He started collecting antiques and spent more time with his grandchildren. He read *The New York Times* at his desk and, most incredible of all, he and his wife took vacations.

Notwithstanding Murray's less-than-enthusiastic participation, Zabar's continued to prosper as New York City's financial situation kept improving and real estate values skyrocketed. Zabar's was now serving twenty-five thousand customers per week and employing two hundred people. This was the era of Reaganomics, as portrayed in Tom Wolfe's novel *The Bonfire of the Vanities* and in Oliver Stone's film *Wall Street*. The Upper West Side somehow managed to remain a mixed neighborhood economically. Despite the onslaught of high-earning young professionals, there were still elderly on fixed budgets in rent-controlled apartments, working-class families in the Mitchell-Lama housing projects, and low-income residents in the tenements that lined some of the side streets. Crack cocaine dealers were everywhere, and street crime continued to be a problem. It was a challenging environment, but Zabar's was able to navigate it.

Murray kept trying to maintain his vow to arrive at the store much later than his customary 6:00 a.m., but he simply couldn't resist showing up well before Zabar's opened to customers. On a typical weekend morning, in all weather, customers started to line up at 8:00 a.m., even though the store didn't open until 9:00 a.m. Many of the employees had been there since 6:00, prepping for the crowds. Packaged goods had to be restocked and the salesclerks had to be sure the croissants and *pains au chocolat* were ready to start baking in the middle of the store, filling the air with the fragrance of browning butter and sugar. Murray would stand at the front, the all-seeing stage manager listening and looking as the door buzzer continuously signaled deliveries of freshly baked bagels and breads, and as the staff arrived and checked in. Finally, just before 9:00, all the employees would take to their stations, readying themselves for the onslaught. The line outside was long and restive. One of the managers would check his watch and call out, "Thirty seconds! Everybody ready?" Then, as the doors were opened, about one hundred people would rush through, racing toward the take-a-number machines at the appetizing, deli meat, and cheese departments. The trick was to take numbers for all three at the same time and then simultaneously monitor the progress at each counter. Somehow, it all worked. Under Murray's command, on Sundays Zabar's grossed more than $100,000.

To keep up with all this increasing activity, the store kept expanding within the space that it had acquired back in 1978. And so in 1990, the Zabar's bread department was officially moved into the store's northernmost building. This was the old 2249 Broadway address, where, in 1934, Louis and Lilly first rented that counter to sell smoked fish and deli meat, and decided to call their little store Zabar's.

Throughout the expansions and the dramas being played out

among Saul, Stanley, and Murray, my brother, David, had been learning the ropes. David had been working at Zabar's since he was thirteen, and upon his graduation in 1982 from Rochester Institute of Technology, he became a full-time employee. He and his wife, Tracey, had a six-month-old son, Benjamin, when David started at the cheese counter. Two years later, he became Saul's apprentice in the appetizing and coffee departments. Among the fish he was responsible for purchasing was herring. No one in our family is a big fan of herring, so David had to learn to like it. Herring is popular in Scandinavia and the Netherlands, but in America it became known as a Jewish food, mainly because it was a plentiful and inexpensive source of protein for the poverty-stricken Eastern European Jews who immigrated to this country in the early decades of the twentieth century and remembered it from the "old country." Back in Louis's day, a pickled herring and a slice of pumpernickel bread was a meal. It was still a favorite of Murray Klein's for lunch or a snack. In a 1989 *New York Times* article about pickled herring for Hanukkah, my brother told Joan Nathan, a renowned cookbook author and authority on Jewish cuisine, "When I stick my hand in the barrels to feel the plumpness of the herring, I feel like I am going back to the time of my grandfather."

There are many kinds of herring, and many ways to prepare it. The Jewish herring tradition began with schmaltz (which means fat in German and Yiddish) herring, a mature herring that contains at least 18 percent fat and comes from the North Atlantic. At Nova Scotia Food Products, the wholesaler in East Williamsburg, Brooklyn, where he chose whole schmaltz herrings from Iceland, David gave each one a gentle squeeze to make sure it was plump enough. He bought fifty pounds of schmaltz herring per week. After his selection arrived at Zabar's, the schmaltz herring was sugar-cured in vegetable oil, then cut at the counter and sold with sliced onions and more oil.

Another type of herring, which comes from Newfoundland, is used to make the old-fashioned pickled herring that the store sells. This "dressed" salt-cured herring—including the skin and bones but with the head and tail removed—is soaked in water to remove some of the salt; marinated in a strong brine of white vinegar, sugar, water, and spices for a week; and then marinated for another week in a weaker brine. Saul and David regularly sampled the herring in this marinade to make sure the balance of salt, sugar, and vinegar was correct. Once the process was complete, the old-fashioned pickled herring was cut into chunks and sold by weight at the appetizing counter, in a clear sauce with onions and bay leaves. David would purchase eighty pounds of herring each week for this recipe.

Skinless Canadian salt herring fillets were pickled in the same way as the old-fashioned pickled herring and then sold in either a

My brother, David, Zabar's executive director, has worked at the store for his entire career, in many capacities. (WILLIE ZABAR/COPYRIGHT © ZABAR'S AND COMPANY, INC. ALL RIGHTS RESERVED.)

cream sauce made with sour cream, onions, vinegar, and sugar or a clear sauce with onions and the weaker brine. All told, Zabar's buys about two barrels (220 pounds net weight per barrel) of Canadian herring per week.

Other herring products sold at Zabar's include matjes (Dutch for maiden, or young), which is made from female herring from the Netherlands, Sweden, or Iceland that is cured in salt and sugar and sold in wine sauce with onions and dill, and a salad made of chopped herring mixed with vinegar, celery, salt, mayonnaise, onions, and applesauce.

With the partners' blessing, David also introduced something quite revolutionary at Zabar's in the mid-1980s. The appetizing specialties and cooked prepared foods had always been sold by salesclerks manning the counters, but at Tracey's urging, David installed a self-service refrigerated case filled with the store's signature products, including packaged smoked salmon, herring, chopped liver, soups, and salads. It was a big hit, and Zabar's customers who prefer to grab and go rather than stand in line for personal service were even more delighted when the offerings later expanded to include hundreds of other products.

Like other high-level employees at Zabar's, David often worked sixty hours a week and on major holidays. His days sometimes began at 4:00 a.m., when the smoked fish houses opened and he had to select and/or approve what the store would be ordering that day. Saul had no compunction about calling him—and other employees—at home at all hours of the night and on weekends. When David requested more time with his family and fewer off-hours intrusions, Saul refused, and so David left in January 1992. A few months later, Saul regretted what he'd done and asked David to come back, but David stayed away for about a year. When he returned, he chose to work behind the scenes, in administration, an area of the business with more regular hours.

As the 1990s progressed, some of the store's key employees began to retire. Harold Horowytz, the manager of the deli department who had been Stanley's accomplice in all those taste tests, retired in 1992, at age sixty-four, after twenty years at Zabar's. Harold moved with his wife to New Bern, North Carolina, but he didn't entirely sever his connection to Zabar's. Each fall, in preparation for the holiday season, Harold would plant himself at his kitchen table sometime in October and begin calling the meat suppliers, conferencing in Saul to set prices for the hams, roasted turkeys, garlic chickens, racks of lamb, poached salmon, and brisket that Zabar's would be ordering. He did all of this without a computer or email, and he wrote nothing down. The entire delicatessen inventory and all the prices were in his head. Then, a few weeks before Thanksgiving, Harold would drive up from North Carolina to work his old shift. From 6:00 a.m. to 4:00 p.m., he stood in his white coat behind the meat counter, next to the knishes and the strudels. He tasted the pastrami to make sure it wasn't too rubbery or salty, and he made sure the sides of beef were sliced perfectly. Wise, respected, and beloved by the entire staff and by his loyal customers, Harold never missed a Zabar's holiday selling season—eventually helped along by a pacemaker and a new left knee—until he died in May 2016, at age eighty-eight.

Sometimes, the most dedicated employees are the ones who come to work at the store after successful careers in other areas. A few years after Harold retired, Len Berk took on slicing fish at Zabar's as a part-time second career, after retiring as a certified public accountant in 1994. He has said that he never felt more appreciated or admired. When I was a child, the entire appetizing staff was Jewish. In later years, several Chinese men were hired; at Zabar's today, most of the slicers are Latino. Len, who calls himself the last Jewish lox slicer at Zabar's, finds joy in educating his customers about fish and in serving celebrities such as Itzhak Perlman. But most of all, Len loves the act of slicing salmon. In an article he wrote for the *Forward,* he described "carefully cutting away that deliciously chewy surface of the 'side,' exposing the glossy undersurface of the fish, removing the pin bones with needle nose pliers, and gliding my vinyl-gloved hand back and forth over its oily surface—a truly sensuous experience." Like the surfer in perpetual search for that perfect wave, Len is always working toward achieving that perfect slice. (With great sadness, Len was furloughed by Zabar's in April 2020; at age ninety, he was at the highest risk for contracting COVID-19. But as of May 2021, Len—

now fully vaccinated—is back behind the counter, slicing away, to everyone's delight.)

THE PARTNERS' LONG-STANDING conflict over Murray's desire to retire finally came to a head in 1994. It began with Murray suing Saul and Stanley in New York State Supreme Court. He wanted to force them into arbitration over his demand that they buy him out of his share of the business for $6 million or, alternatively, sell their shares to him for $12 million. With Zabar's valued at $18 million and grossing $39 million a year, Saul and Stanley could easily afford to pay Murray the $6 million he was asking for. But because this wasn't part of their partnership agreement, they refused to do so, contending that Murray had the option to retire while remaining a co-owner. Murray rejected this idea, fearing that the value of Zabar's would decline after his retirement. Saul and Stanley countered that if Murray was so concerned about the economic future of Zabar's, he should have trained a new general manager to assume his role. But they knew that no employee could fill Murray's shoes. In fact, in their court papers, Saul and Stanley claimed that "upon Klein's retirement as the key man, in effect its chief operating officer, the business will seriously decline in value." In addition to their concern about the potential decline in value of Zabar's, Saul and Stanley knew that if Murray retired, they would have to increase their responsibilities beyond their comfort zones, as well as increase their workloads. Neither wanted to arrive at the store every morning at 6:00 a.m. and, on top of what they were already doing, manage two hundred employees, day in and day out. Another consideration was that my father needed to continue to set aside time to manage his real estate company. Of course, Saul and Stanley knew that Murray was not going to live forever, but they wanted to put off his inevitable departure for as long as they could. In their view, it was a marriage that had indeed gone bad years earlier, but it was at least a known quantity. All three men were stubborn. The media was having a field day with the story, but the food world was on tenterhooks.

Ultimately, Saul and Stanley caved. Murray, now seventy-two,

had finally worn them down. On October 19, 1994, Zabar's announced that Murray Klein had sold his share of the store to Saul
and Stanley and would stay on as a part-time consultant. The day
after the announcement, Murray and Edith left for a Mediterranean
cruise. "I'm a millionaire," he told *New York Times* reporter Bryan
Miller, "so I have to spend the money fast."

Murray did, in the end, get to enjoy his retirement. He died on
December 7, 2007, at the age of eighty-four. His obituary in *The
New York Times* described him as "the public face of Zabar's . . .
who helped transform Zabar's from a typical Jewish delicatessen
on the Upper West Side of Manhattan into a culinary and cultural
landmark."

While Saul and Stanley were fighting with Murray over his retirement, Eli was developing his business on the East Side of Manhattan. The Henri Bendel outpost of E.A.T. had closed in 1985, the
same year Eli began an enterprise that would revolutionize the
bread industry in the tristate area. For the smoked salmon sandwiches sold at E.A.T., Eli wanted to produce the kind of artisanal
bread he had tasted at Poilâne bakery in Paris and at the small
family bakeries he had visited in the French countryside. He began
baking bread at E.A.T. and not only using it for his sandwiches
but also selling it to local restaurants such as Tavern on the Green
and the Oyster Bar at Grand Central Terminal. After much trial and
error, Eli created the sourdough bread of his dreams: one with
lots of crust, a sour taste like the Jewish corn rye of his childhood,
and a tight texture. Eli's artisanal breads were a huge success and
inspired many bakers in the greater New York area to establish
their own businesses.

In 1990, Eli married an elegant woman named Devon Fredericks,
whose calm demeanor and seriousness of purpose were a good
balance for her husband's energetic, restless nature. Devon had her
own foodie bona fides as a private chef, caterer, and cofounder and
former owner of the legendary Loaves and Fishes gourmet food
store in Sagaponack, Long Island.

Devon became the quiet, creative force behind what was rap-
idly expanding into a food empire. Eli's next step was to open
Eli's Bread, a 15,000-square-foot bakery on East Ninety-First Street,

Eli in 2005, at one of the stores in his
Upper East Side food empire. (ELIZABAR.COM)

which became the source of hearth-baked breads, rolls, focaccias, and bagels for one thousand restaurants, hotels, and stores, including Fairway, Balducci's, Grace's Marketplace, and Zabar's. Next door to the bakery, at The Vinegar Factory, a grocery store and café, he brilliantly pioneered the concept of recycling unsold fresh products into cooked prepared food. Then he opened up yet another culinary frontier in 1995, when he became New York City's first commercial rooftop gardener, growing salad greens and tomatoes in greenhouses he'd built on the roof of The Vinegar Factory.

Eli's restless energy, so reminiscent of his father's, continues to propel him through long work hours and an endless stream of new ideas, bold ventures, and audacious business plans. And he does it all garbed in his trademark outfit of one collared shirt on top of another, a down vest, corduroy pants, sneakers, and a gray knitted watch cap. A casual observer—not realizing the shirts are custom-made in Paris—might mistake him for a kitchen hand.

ALONGSIDE THE EXCITEMENT generated by the ongoing success of Zabar's and of Eli's various enterprises, the passage of time brought with it the sad recognition that other types of changes were in the offing. At some point in the early 1980s, Mark and I flew to Miami Beach to visit Grandma Lilly, expecting her to greet us with her customary "Have you eaten yet? Can I fix you something?" But this time, she confessed with some embarrassment that she had bought no food for us. In the fridge there was only milk, cottage cheese, and two oranges. Mark and I were puzzled by the fact that, most uncharacteristically, there wasn't enough food in her apartment to sustain even one person, but we took her grocery shopping, and all seemed fine.

Then, one evening a few months later in Mohegan Colony, Lilly walked from her house to my parents' house next door, climbed the stairs to the porch, and peered through the screen.

"Lilly, come in!" my mother called out.

"I just want to look in," said Lilly. She stood for a while, motionless, just staring straight into my parents' kitchen.

"Lilly, you can't just stand there," my mother said with some exasperation. "Please come in! You're making me crazy!" But my grandmother would not move, eventually turning around and returning to her house. This scenario repeated itself on several occasions throughout the summer.

Grandma Lilly was by then in her early eighties, and we chalked those incidents up to the eccentricities of old age. When she began to misplace things—most frequently, her handbag—we thought this was just the increased anxiety that came with her advancing years.

It eventually became apparent to us all that Grandma Lilly could no longer live by herself, but she was furious when my parents hired a middle-aged caregiver named Susan. Lilly hated having what she called a "stranger" in her house who told her what to do, instead of the other way around. Susan bore the brunt of Lilly's displeasure for as long as she could; many other caregivers followed. Lilly called them all "Susan."

As my grandmother's dementia progressed, Saul and Stanley felt they needed to be close by to supervise her care. She could not spend winters in Miami, and her sons moved her to The Bromley on Broadway and Eighty-Third Street, where she was tended to by two shifts of caregivers. Then one day Saul came to visit, but Lilly didn't recognize him.

"I'm Saul, your son," he said.

"Well, if you came more often, I'd know who you are," she retorted. It was somewhat reassuring to see that there was still a bit of the old Lilly left in her.

Another time, my mother ran into Lilly and her caregiver on Broadway.

"Nice young girl, you look familiar," Lilly said to my mother.

"Lilly, do you know who I am? I'm Judy."

"Are you married?" Lilly responded.

"Oh, yes, to Stanley, your son."

"Does he make a good living?"

"Yes, he works in the store, Zabar's."

"Do you have children?"

"Yes. Lori, David, and Sandy."

Even in the advanced stages of dementia, Grandma Lilly was fully cognizant of what made life meaningful. Back when she was in full command of her faculties, she would have added, "I only want for my children to be happy," which was her way of explaining what results when you make a good living, are married, and have children.

Then there was the time when Grandma Lilly somehow managed to escape from her caregiver and wander down Broadway from Eighty-Third Street to Sixty-Fifth Street, near Lincoln Center. When a bystander tried to help, all she could do was repeat, "I'm Mrs. Zabar! I'm Mrs. Zabar!" Finally, a policeman brought her to the store. "Does anyone know this woman?" he asked doubtfully. "She says she's Mrs. Zabar."

"She *is* Mrs. Zabar," David told him. "She's my grandmother."

Sadly, Lilly's cognitive decline continued, and then her body gave out, on December 22, 1995—by some uncanny coincidence, the day she traditionally celebrated her birthday. Over the decades, she had succeeded in keeping up the two-year shave-off of her age that she'd initiated when she applied for her marriage license back in 1927, as well as the additional year that she'd trimmed off when she became a United States citizen in 1928. In a final triumph, she was even able to throw posthumous smoke on the fact-checkers at *The New York Times,* who had to let stand in her obituary that "she was ninety, or perhaps ninety-two or ninety-three." In addition to Lilly's enormous role in my life and in the lives of everyone in our family, she made a lasting and much broader impact as a founder and partner in Zabar's. Her achievements were officially recognized in *The Women Who Made New York,* a very interesting book by Julie Scelfo that was published in 2016.

My grandmother's death did not come as a shock to us; it was more like a gradual departure from our world. I had already been mourning the loss of her for years. The Schrafft's that Grandma Lilly took me to as a child is long gone, the building now occupied by a Barnes & Noble. But when I pass by, I think of my special Saturdays with my grandmother, when we ate coffee ice cream and discussed everything. I hope I inherited her best qualities: warmth, generosity, hospitality, charisma, and joy.

Lilly Zabar's Chopped Liver

Edited and tested by Monita Buchwald

Grandma Lilly's chopped liver, served as a *forshpeis* (appetizer) with crackers or challah on Shabbat and Jewish holidays, was beloved by us all. The version at Zabar's is very much like hers—hearty, rich, and filling. When my brother, David, introduced refrigerated prepacked Zabar's specialties, he made sure that chopped liver would be one of the items available for customers who want to grab and go. It continues to be a very popular item in the store. I always laugh when someone feeling ignored or regarded as inferior quips, "What am I, chopped liver?" Chopped liver is a delicious, traditional Jewish food, and there's nothing inferior about it.

MAKES 2½ CUPS; SERVES 6

INGREDIENTS

1 large sweet onion, sliced

⅓ cup schmaltz (chicken fat) or vegetable oil, or more to taste; schmaltz can be purchased or rendered (see page 170)

1 pound chicken livers

3 tablespoons Madeira or marsala wine

2 large hard-boiled eggs

Kosher salt

Freshly ground black pepper

Crackers, challah, or matzoh for serving

DIRECTIONS

1. Sauté the onion in about half of the schmaltz in a large frying pan over medium-high heat until golden, about 8 minutes. Remove the onion together with the liquid from the pan and set aside.

2. Add the remaining schmaltz and the chicken livers to the pan. Cook, turning the livers until only a slight amount of pink shows when the liver is cut, about 5 minutes.

3. Add the wine and cook over high heat until the chicken livers are cooked through and the liquid has reduced by half. There should be just enough liquid to moisten the livers; they should be soft (not hard) and well done.

4. Traditionally, the onion, livers, and their juices are then put into a wooden bowl and chopped with a hand chopper—which is why the end result is called, in Yiddish, *gehackter* (chopped) liver. Alternatively, place the onion, livers, and their juices in a food processor. Process carefully until they reach the desired texture.

5. Remove the liver mixture from the food processor and place in a medium bowl.

6. Place the hard-boiled eggs in the food processor and process until coarsely chopped. (Or you can chop the hard-boiled eggs with a hand chopper.) Add the chopped hard-boiled eggs to the liver mixture in the bowl. Stir to combine. Add salt, pepper, and additional schmaltz to taste.

7. Chill and serve as a first course or appetizer with crackers, challah, or matzoh.

How to Render Your Own Schmaltz

Pull the skin off four or five 4-pound raw chickens and pull as much of the fat as you can from inside their cavities. Slice the skin and the fat into small pieces, put it all into the freezer in a plastic bag, and let it freeze. Put the frozen skin and fat into a small frying pan over medium heat; add salt and cook until the fat is melted and the skin turns a deep golden brown (but is not burned). The crispy pieces of fried skin are called gribenes. Strain the fat through a small sieve, and that's your schmaltz. If you can restrain yourself from munching them all up, you can chop the gribenes together with the liver.

10

Zabar's Present Tense

THE MOVIE *YOU'VE GOT MAIL*, WHICH STARRED TOM HANKS AND MEG Ryan and was directed by Nora Ephron, was a big hit when it was released during the holiday season of 1998. A lot of it was filmed on location on the Upper West Side, so it was a boon for the neighborhood as well. Local landmarks such as Barney Greengrass, the West 79th Street Boat Basin, Gray's Papaya, Cafe Lalo, Starbucks, the Ninety-First Street garden in Riverside Park, and H&H Bagels (which is now a Verizon store) each got a bit of screen time, but only Zabar's got an entire scene. By charming the cashier, Hanks's character comes to the rescue of Ryan's character when she finds herself with just a Visa credit card in the cash-only checkout line, right in the middle of the store's pre-Thanksgiving crush.

Ephron had to lobby hard to persuade Saul to allow her to film in Zabar's. She finally won him over by agreeing to start shooting at 7:00 p.m., after the store closed, and to be out by 6:00 a.m. the next morning. If she went over the allotted time, she would have to pay Zabar's $5,000 for every fifteen minutes of overtime. Ephron and her crew made sure to be done by 6:00 a.m. Scott Goldshine, Zabar's general manager, appeared in *You've Got Mail* as an extra, and to this day, he smiles when he overhears customers talking about the movie.

Busy young professionals with families continued to flood into the Upper West Side, and they wanted to purchase prepared food and everything to go with it, all in one place. Zabar's, Fairway, and Citarella stepped up to fulfill the demand. Beginning in the late 1990s, Zabar's added organic greens flown in from California, sold salads in containers, and increased its selection of prepackaged cooked foods. Russian Jewish immigrant Boris Bassin, the head chef at Zabar's for more than thirty years, produced nearly two hundred types of cooked dishes per day for sale behind the counter and two hundred varieties of prepared foods that were available in the self-service refrigerated cases. Citarella, known for its fresh fish, added a butcher, prepared foods, fresh pasta, deli, smoked fish, and groceries. Fairway, traditionally known for its great values in produce, had already expanded to cheese, bread, fish, meat, and premade foods. Those six blocks on Broadway, from Seventy-Fourth Street to Eightieth Street, became the epicenter of a new national trend for high-quality prepared foods.

Around this time, another Zabar joined the staff. In her midtwenties, my cousin Ann Zabar, Saul and Carole's oldest child, became her father's right hand. One of her jobs was to taste every shipment of caviar that entered the store. In the 1990s, most caviar sold in the United States still came from Russia, from the Caspian Sea. But because of overfishing and pollution, Russian beluga sturgeon was eventually designated an endangered species and Russian beluga caviar was banned from sale in the United States in 2005.

Ann tasted the caviar when it arrived in two-kilo tins and tasted it again when it was repacked into small tins for sale behind the appetizing counter. By 1998, Zabar's was one of the largest retailers of caviar in the country, selling more than five thousand pounds every year. Three-fifths of that caviar is sold during the holiday season, from Thanksgiving to New Year's.

Ann was as fastidious as her father when it came to tasting. On a tasting day, she avoided coffee, onions, and anything peppery or tart, such as lemons, so that her ability to gauge the saltiness of the eggs would not become distorted. All of Zabar's caviar is malossol (the Russian word for slightly salted); the trick is for the caviar to have the precisely correct amount of salt. Too much overpowers the taste of the caviar and too little makes it taste mild and bland.

When Ann tasted a sample, she measured the texture of the sturgeon roe by pressing the tiny eggs against the roof of her mouth. They should be firm without being crunchy, and they should not pop the way salmon caviar eggs do. The aroma of the caviar is important, too: it should smell like the sea.

Caviar comes in three types: osetra, sevruga, and beluga. Ann's favorite, osetra, has a hint of a fruity-nutty flavor and is brownish to yellowish in color. It comes from midsize sturgeon, a fish that is, on average, ten feet long and weighs about 500 pounds. Saul prefers sevruga's tiny, gray-to-black eggs, which come from the smallest sturgeon—about seven feet long and 150 pounds. Today, most osetra caviar is sustainably farmed in countries all over the world. My preference has always been for wild beluga, the rarest and most expensive. Beluga eggs range from silvery gray to black and come from the largest sturgeon, which can be twenty feet long and weigh more than a ton. But because these sturgeons are found only in the Caspian Sea, wild beluga caviar has not been sold in the United States since 2005.

During the Christmas to New Year's season, the demand for caviar is so great that Zabar family members—spouses as well as children—and former employees are asked to pitch in as temporary salesclerks. In December 1999, Saul's wife, Carole, returned for a stint as the Caviar Lady alongside former employee Eddie Berrios. Carole found watching customers order caviar fascinating. The more experienced would order fourteen-ounce tins of beluga without hesitation, but others stood hesitantly at the counter because they knew nothing about caviar and worried that they might make an expensive mistake. Usually the latter were buying caviar as a gift for someone else and begged the employee behind the counter for an on-the-spot education, despite the impatient hordes waiting behind them. In their anxiety, these customers sometimes overshared. "One woman confided in me that she was buying the caviar for a sister-in-law whom she detested," Carole wrote in the Zabar's newsletter after her stint in 1999, "and therefore it was doubly important that she get the best."

That year, disaster struck two days before Christmas: a major shipment of caviar from one of the store's largest suppliers was delayed, and Zabar's actually ran out of their prime caviar: wild-caught osetra and beluga. People were already on edge with fears of a global electronic meltdown at midnight on December 31, 1999, when computers all over the world were supposed to seamlessly flip over to 2000. What should have been a minor caviar disappointment had customers up in arms. One young woman was so afraid of disappointing her boyfriend that she began to cry. All Carole could do was suggest that people either return to the store the next day, when the caviar was supposed to arrive, or buy sevruga or pasteurized osetra instead.

Twenty years later, on December 30, 2019, I took a number on the caviar line, and I was delighted to see a member of the fourth generation of the Zabar family—David's youngest son, Willie—working behind the counter, alongside Eddie Berrios, who, at age sixty-six, still returns to help out every holiday season. I purchased the smallest size of imported farmed Siberian osetra, which Willie assured me was the best osetra the store carried. I was impressed by my twenty-six-year-old nephew's expertise and couldn't help but wish that Louis and Lilly were still around to watch their great-grandson serve the customers.

But for all the people splurging on caviar on the now-prosperous Upper West Side, many of the store's neighbors were struggling to put food on their tables. Distressed by what they were seeing around them, Saul and Stanley became involved in neighborhood and food-related charities. My father joined the board of Careers Through Culinary Arts Program, an organization that raises money to fund education and jobs in the food industry for disadvantaged young people. Saul and Stanley also supported C-CAP's annual benefit, at which famous chefs cooked for the guests and a silent auction was held. In 2001, my father bid on and won a lunch for six with Julia Child at the legendary restaurant Le Cirque; it was donated by the restaurant's owner, Sirio Maccioni. On June 13, my parents; my sister, Sandy; her husband, Ira; Mark; and I sat at Le Cirque with Sirio and Julia's press agent, Fern Berman, making small talk while we waited for Julia's delayed shuttle flight to arrive from Boston. She was graciously coming to New York City just for this lunch with us. Julia walked through the door, tall and erect despite her reliance on a walker. She apologized for her lateness and immediately began peppering us with questions—"Stanley, how is business? Sirio, what sort of food are people eating in New York City restaurants?"—before launching into one of her favorite

Longtime Zabar's chef Boris Bassin, Julia Child, and Saul,
during Julia's memorable visit to the store in 2001. (STANLEY ZABAR)

topics. "There is nothing wrong with *butter*!" she exclaimed. "Why are people so afraid of *butter*? It makes food taste *good*!"

As the meal ended, Julia mentioned that she had never been to Zabar's. My parents asked if she had time for a visit after lunch, and she said that she did. When my parents and Julia arrived at the store, every single person there, customers and employees alike, instantly recognized Julia. But no one interrupted her visit. As she walked through the aisles and past the counters, people simply smiled and nodded in acknowledgment and then stepped back in awe, as if in the presence of royalty.

Julia died three years after that lunch, in 2004, at age ninety-two. I think she was the most influential person in the food world during my lifetime. She certainly influenced Zabar's: her success in educating Americans about food and opening them up to new tastes and culinary experiences is one of the reasons why Zabar's expanded the range of products and kitchen equipment they sold. And it was thanks to her that there were customers who were interested in buying what was being stocked. Julia's legacy lives on.

Zabar's is also a major supporter of Symphony Space, an Upper West Side performing arts and cultural center. My father and I have served on their board of directors, and since 2007, Zabar's has sponsored Symphony Space's Selected Shorts program, an annual series in which stage and screen actors read classic and new short fiction before a live audience. It's also broadcast throughout the United States on public radio. In April 2005, Symphony Space honored Saul and Stanley at their annual gala. The late Isaiah Sheffer, a founder and artistic director of Symphony Space, wrote a song in honor of the occasion, which was performed by the actor and singer Liz Callaway. Here are some excerpts from "The Zabar Mystique":

> *I met him in Zabar's*
> *On the Upper West Side.*
> *He was a gentile,*
> *I tried to show my best side.*
> *"Nix on the belly-lox, friend,*
> *It's too salty," I said.*
> *"Try the Nova instead."*
> *I'd made a friend . . . in Zabar's.*
>
> *We wandered away*
> *To the duck cassoulet.*
> *And held hands by the time*
> *We reached freeze-dried quinces.*
> *Till finally we kissed,*
> *Under the blintzes.*
>
> *The Zabar Mystique*
> *Was warming our chèvre.*
> *My kippered heart would love*
> *This whitefish for-evre.*

The song may be tongue-in-cheek, but the Zabar mystique is no myth. Customers have indeed met, flirted, and proposed in the store. In a 2017 podcast interview on *Eater Upsell,* Jessica Seinfeld recalled a visit to Zabar's early in her relationship with Jerry, when he turned to her in front of the appetizing counter and said, "This is the perfect time to tell you that I love you." A lifelong Zabar's customer, Jessica remembers thinking at the time, "My grandmother

"Hi there! Didn't we meet at Zabar's?"

"The Zabar Mystique" of romantic possibility was even the subject of a New Yorker *cartoon, by Donald Reilly, which ran in the June 9, 1975, issue.* (DONALD REILLY/ THE NEW YORKER, © CONDÉ NAST)

would be so happy." Now Jessica's children accompany her to the appetizing counter while her husband waits outside in the car. Like Nora Ephron, Jessica considers Zabar's family.

Zabar's also got a mention in the very first episode of the streaming television series *The Marvelous Mrs. Maisel*. When Miriam tells her father that Joel just left her, he says, "You need a husband." To which she responds, "What am I supposed to do, go buy one at Zabar's?" According to Wikipedia, a partial list of the television programs on which Zabar's has either been mentioned or has appeared in includes *Northern Exposure, Will & Grace, How I Met Your Mother, Mad About You, Friends, Sex and the City, The Nanny, The Simpsons, The West Wing, 30 Rock, The Daily Show, The Colbert Report, Episodes, Law & Order, Saturday Night Live, Gossip Girl,* and *Broad City.*

One of my favorite mentions was in a 2019 *Saturday Night Live* skit, "Michael Cohen Hearings," in which Kate McKinnon as Congresswoman Debbie Wasserman Schultz declares, "Mr. Cohen, for this portion of the hearing, I would like us both to lean into our New York accents so hard that our viewers will think they are stuck in line at Zabar's."

While it's certainly fun to be part of American popular culture, this media presence also probably helps drive Zabar's ever-growing online business. Zabars.com went live in 2002, and to date it makes up 20 percent of the store's sales. Online customers include people who grew up in New York City and moved away or lived in the city for a period of time and left, those who experienced Zabar's as tourists, and others who have never entered the store but became hooked when they received one or more of Zabar's products in the mail as a gift. These members of the Zabar's diaspora buy online from the store because they appreciate the quality that comes with the brand, because they are nostalgic for their childhood deli and appetizing experiences, because they want to maintain their connection to New York City, or because buying Zabar's products helps them maintain their Jewish identity.

In a 2012 *New Yorker* article about New York's food megastores entitled "A Bushel and a Peck," Patricia Marx affectionately likens each store to a house of worship belonging to a specific denomination. She called Zabar's "the Orthodox congregation of comestibles that is beloved by nearly all." She then went on to describe Eli's Manhattan as "St. Eli's Cathedral . . . A secessionist sect founded in 2000 by Eli Zabar, . . . these latter-day Episcopalians figured out how to profit from slicing up stale bagels and packaging them as bagel chips." But she also reported, "Prepared food, such as balsamic chicken, are made perfectly; soups are tasty . . . And on the seventh day Eli created homemade potato chips."

MANY MEMBERS OF THE Zabar family are involved in the visual arts as professionals, amateurs, or collectors, so the clan was delighted when street art and Zabar's had a happy encounter on the Upper West Side. In 2013, the famous British graffiti artist known pseudonymously as Banksy announced that he would hold a one-month art "residency" in New York City. From October 1 through October 31, Banksy created one piece of outdoor artwork per day, in what he styled as an art show on the streets of New York that he called *Better Out Than In*. This caused plenty of excitement because the site of each work was a surprise and could be located only through a daily clue provided by Banksy on social media. On Sunday, October 20, my mother received a call in Mohegan Colony from a newspaper reporter who told her that on the side of a building owned by our family on the northeast corner of Broadway and Seventy-Ninth Street, Banksy had spray-painted a silhouette of a boy holding a raised mallet poised to strike an actual New York City Fire Department Siamese connection. The reporter wanted to know what we were going to do about it. My mother quite reasonably asked him what he thought we should do about it, and he said it should be protected before other graffiti artists tagged it. My mother consulted with my father, who huddled with Saul on the phone. They came up with the idea of shielding the artwork with a sheet of Plexiglas, and Saul promptly marched over to the building with two Zabar's employees to protect our Banksy. "It's fabulous," he told the *New York Post* reporter. "It's not graffiti. It's really artistic. I'd like him to do more work on the building. I'd be delighted. It's fun. The kids were putting their heads on the [stand]pipe, participating in the art. People are interacting and reacting—it's really street theater." Not all New Yorkers were as pleased as we were by Banksy's work. Shortly thereafter, another graffiti artist spray-painted LET THE STREET DECIDE on the Plexiglas. Mayor Michael Bloomberg declared Banksy's art to be vandalism. The press reported that the New York City Police Department was hunting for him.

Our Banksy is the only work from the artist's *Better Out Than In* series that is still visible to the public. The other twenty-nine (the artwork scheduled for October 23 was canceled due to "police activity") have been stolen, removed, or covered up. Tripadvisor lists viewing our Banksy as number 320 of "1,325 Things to Do in New York City." Because all thirty of Banksy's New York City artworks were captured on social media, they are viewable in the excellent 2014 HBO documentary *Banksy Does New York,* directed by Chris Moukarbel. In it, Saul and Zabar's get a nice few minutes of screen time.

IN ADDITION TO FOOD and housewares, Zabar's does a brisk business in what we refer to as "wearables" and "other Zabar's gear." These items, all of them emblazoned with the Zabar's logo, include shopping bags, T-shirts, aprons, mugs, tote bags, sweatshirts, oven mitts, and the beloved Zabar's baseball cap (my father never leaves home without it). A customer who lives on a kibbutz in Israel and visits Zabar's whenever he is in New York even wore his Zabar's baseball cap to his daughter's wedding instead of a yarmulke. It's impossible not to feel honored by that.

My grandparents had always encouraged their family to visit Israel, the Jewish homeland that they had supported so ardently in their lifetimes, and in March 2009, fourteen of us traveled there on a family trip. Our group consisted of my parents; Mark and myself; our children, Henry and Marguerite; my sister, Sandy, and her husband, Ira Breite; their children, Noah and Josh; Eli and Devon; and their twin sons, Sasha and Oliver. (Unlike the rest of us, Saul and Carole had been to Israel many times before, so an introductory sightseeing trip was not something they were interested in.) The moment I entered Jerusalem, I wondered why I had waited so long to do this. The buildings, old and new, were clad in glowing, creamy yellow Jerusalem stone that gave the city an aura of timeless beauty and history. We explored the usual tourist sites—the Western Wall, Jerusalem's Jewish Quarter, The Israel Museum, the Church of the Holy Sepulchre, Masada, the Dead Sea, and the oasis Ein Gedi—and a visit to Yad Vashem, Israel's memorial to the Holocaust, was an emotional experience for us all.

A particular highlight of the trip was a visit to a place that seemed to be made to order for our family: the Machane Yehuda Market in Jerusalem. It looked like Zabar's on some crazy form of Israeli steroids. Open booths were piled high with colorful spices, candies, dried fruits, cookies, and vegetables. Along the edges of the market were small stores with arched entrances, specializing in meats, fish, poultry, and bread. As Mark and I were walking along, admiring the bounty, I heard Sandy yell, "Eli, there's a bread bakery!" By the time we turned around, Eli, Sasha, Oliver, Sandy, Ira, and their boys were all standing behind the counter of the small white-tiled shop, deep in conversation with the owner and his workers. They were enthusiastically prodding the mounds of dough in flour-covered wooden trays, learning how to roll it out, and tasting the round, fragrant disks of golden-brown pita as they emerged from the oven. There was no mistaking that look in Eli's eyes as he thoughtfully licked the last crumbs from his fingers. I could just see him teaching his bakers how to make artisanal pita at his bread factory back home.

Our final destination that day was Rosh Pina, a small town in northern Israel. Our entourage took over the stone-vaulted Chocolata restaurant for dinner with twenty-two of our Israeli cousins, descendants of Louis's sister Gittel, some of whom we were meeting for the first time. Devon's Israeli cousins joined our party, too. There were so many of us that we could barely walk between the tables. We all knew that our grandparents would have been delighted by this gathering of the American and Israeli branches of our family.

While we were eating and drinking with our boisterous crowd of cousins, Stanley and Eli decided to alter the next day's itinerary to include a visit to what we humorously refer to as our ancestral parking lot. In 1949, on what proved to be Louis's first and last trip to Israel, Lilly and Louis had purchased land in Nahariya, which was then a developing Israeli resort city along the Mediterranean Sea, just south of the border with Lebanon. Louis had hoped to spend time in Nahariya during the winters, imagining it as Israel's version of Miami Beach, but he died a year later, and the land Louis and Lilly bought became a parking lot. As we gathered there the next day for a family photo, we felt a special connection to Louis and Lilly and the land they loved.

Somewhere along the way I discovered another connection between the Zabars and Israel. In the 1930s, native-born Israelis began to be referred to as sabras, a term derived from the prickly pear cactus that actually originated in Central America and is called *tzabar* in Hebrew. Prickly and tough on the outside but sweet and soft on the inside, the fruit was adopted as the symbol of Israelis who are born into the herculean task of creating a reborn nation on their people's ancient land. My ancestors in Ukraine chose the surname Zabarka in honor of a relative, Rabbi Wolf Zabarska, who emigrated to Palestine in the 1820s. I think this Hebrew spin on our family name brings us full circle from Ukraine to Israel; it certainly would have pleased my grandparents. And from what I have learned about Louis Zabar, the description of the *tzabar* suited him perfectly, too.

Lilly Zabar's Gefilte Fish

Tested and edited by Monita Buchwald

As a little girl, I was surprised one day to find two fish swimming in the bathtub of Grandma Lilly's Upper West Side apartment. They were a carp and a whitefish, and they were destined for her delicious Shabbat gefilte fish. In his magnificent *Encyclopedia of Jewish Food,* the late rabbi and award-winning food historian Gil Marks writes that even as they prospered in America and could afford to buy prepared food, Jewish housewives in the early twentieth century (and some, like Grandma Lilly, for decades thereafter) continued to make their own gefilte fish, as well as to maintain the traditional practice of keeping the carp alive in the bathtub to remove any muddy taste before grinding or chopping up the fillets. While this recipe does not include carp—it can be too earthy for most modern tastes—it is otherwise the basis for the gefilte fish sold at Zabar's today—which, in the store's time-honored manner, melds tradition with current methods and sensibilities.

Since 1992, Eli and Devon have hosted our Zabar family Passover seder in their brownstone on the Upper East Side. The menu features Eli's interpretation of such Passover classics as chopped liver, gefilte fish, chicken soup, and brisket. And each year my father (whose other passion, besides Zabar's, is photography) gathers us together for our three generations group portrait. I know my grandparents would kvell with delight and pride to see their progeny celebrate the Jewish holiday of freedom together.

MAKES 12 PATTIES; SERVES 10 TO 12

*Three generations at our 2016 Passover seder, which has been hosted by
Eli and Devon since 1992. Each year, Stanley (in the white sneakers)
rounds us all up, sets up the camera, and then rushes to the first row
before the shutter clicks.* (STANLEY ZABAR)

INGREDIENTS

For the broth

*Fish heads, bones, and skin from
2 pounds whitefish fillets and
1 pound yellow pike fillets,
thoroughly washed (reserve
the flesh for making the fish
patties: see below)*
2 teaspoons kosher salt

*1 teaspoon freshly ground black
pepper*
1 large onion, sliced
*2 teaspoons sugar, or more to
taste*
*4 to 6 carrots, peeled and sliced
into ½-inch rounds*

For the fish patties

*Flesh from 2 pounds whitefish
fillets*

*Flesh from 1 pound yellow pike
fillets*
1 large egg

1 onion, grated
1 tablespoon kosher salt
½ teaspoon freshly ground black
  pepper

1 tablespoon sugar
¼ cup cold water
2 to 4 tablespoons matzoh meal

Garnish

Grated horseradish for serving   Jellied broth

DIRECTIONS

1. Make the broth: Line a heavy pot with fish heads, bones, and skin. Add the salt, pepper, onion, and sugar.

2. Add enough cold water to cover and bring to a boil.

3. Add the carrots. Reduce the heat to a simmer, and continue to cook the broth while the fish is being prepared.

4. Prepare the fish: Grind the fillets by putting them through the fine blade of a meat grinder twice or chopping them by hand in a wooden bowl. Or you can have the fillets ground at the fish store. You should have about 4 cups ground fish.

5. Combine the ground fish, egg, onion, salt, pepper, and sugar in a large bowl. Add the water and matzoh meal to the mixture, alternating by the spoonful until the texture is light but firm enough to form patties.

6. Remove the fish heads, bones, and skin from the broth. Leave the carrot rounds in.

7. Wet your hands and form the fish mixture into 12 oval patties, about ⅓ cup each. Place the patties gently in the just-simmering broth in one layer. If portions touch, they can be separated later. Simmer, uncovered, for 1½ hours.

8. Place the fish on a large platter or in a large container, along with the carrot rounds. Refrigerate; can be refrigerated up to three days before serving.

9. Strain the broth and place it in a separate container. Chill and let jell.

10. Serve the fish with the carrots, jellied broth, and grated horse-radish.

The Future of Zabar's

SAUL, WHO IS NINETY-THREE AS THIS BOOK IS BEING PUBLISHED AND who never intended to stay at Zabar's when he took charge in 1950 as a twenty-one-year-old, continues to work in the store every day. No one would be more surprised by Saul's devotion to Zabar's than his father, Louis. Stanley, who is now eighty-nine, continues as Saul's hands-on partner. But although they are both in good health for men of their ages, the question becomes more pressing with every passing year: What is the future of Zabar's?

My brother, David, now sixty-five and the store's executive director, has had many roles at Zabar's and knows the business from all sides. Along with the store's longtime dedicated management staff, David will be the link between the old regime and the new. Aaron Zabar, Saul's forty-eight-year-old son, has also been with Zabar's for many years as a front-end manager and will also be part of the family's transition to the next generation.

Until recently, many families in the retail food business wanted their children to become professionals instead, so as to avoid the long hours, hard physical labor, and small profit margins associated with this world. But nowadays, careers in food have become attractive and even hip for people in their twenties and thirties. This is true for our family as well. It's been wonderful to watch as the fourth generation of Zabars—Louis and Lilly's great-grandchildren—enters the food world. Three of David's four sons—Danny, Michael, and Willie—have been working in different areas at Zabar's for several years. Danny has spent time in almost every department and has developed an astonishing expertise in kitchen appliances and gadgets. Michael has been involved in mar-

(From left to right) *David's sons: Danny, Ben, Willie, and Michael Zabar, in 2011. They are members of the fourth generation of Zabars who have worked in the store.* (DAVID ZABAR)

My daughter, Marguerite Zabar Mariscal, and Sandy's sons, Josh and Noah Zabar Breite, had this photo taken for their grandfather Stanley's eighty-fifth birthday in 2017. (SANDY ZABAR)

ket analysis and business administration. And Willie is a content developer for the store's social media accounts, when he isn't performing as a stand-up comedian. Even David's wife, Tracey, is a Zabar's employee. She is the author of a weekly recipe/cookbook blog and giveaway contest on Zabars.com.

Others in the fourth generation will share their expertise as significant advisers. Our daughter, Marguerite Mariscal, now thirty-two, surprised Mark and me when she graduated from Bowdoin College and said she wanted to work in the food world but didn't want to sell food, make it, or serve it. We weren't sure what that left, but she managed to fulfill her goal. After a couple of months working for Eli, Marguerite became a paid communications intern at Momofuku, David Chang's restaurant group. Momofuku then hired her as their social media manager, and she worked her way up to chief executive officer in 2019, at the age of thirty.

My sister Sandy's older son, Noah Breite, caught the food bug while working for Eli one summer between high school and college. Upon graduation from the Cornell University School of Hotel Administration in 2019, Noah entered an executive training program at Restaurant Brands International in Miami, owner of Burger King, Popeyes, and Tim Hortons. It's too soon to say what role Noah will play at Zabar's, but he will undoubtedly bring with him valuable experience from the corporate food world.

Eli's twin sons, Sasha (whose real name is Louis, after his grandfather) and Oliver, have joined their father's empire, which has grown to include Eli's Manhattan, a sprawling 20,000-square-foot store on Third Avenue and Eightieth Street; a few venues at Grand Central Market in Grand Central Terminal; and several Eli's Essentials, grab-and-go shops on the Upper East Side of Manhattan. Under Oliver's guidance, one Eli's Essentials shop is transformed into a craft beer bar in the evenings and another becomes a wine bar. In 2018, Oliver opened Devon NYC (since closed), a cocktail bar and small-plates restaurant on Broome Street on Manhattan's Lower East Side that he named after his mother. Sasha joined him the following year. Oliver and Sasha are now planning the renovation of E.A.T. for its fiftieth anniversary. History comes full circle. Louis and Lilly's descendants will continue to offer customers qual-

For many years, Zabar's has provided complimentary catering for the artists performing at Lincoln Center's Midsummer Night Swing and Lincoln Center Out of Doors. Here's my son, Henry Zabar Mariscal, manning the booth at an event there in 2012.

ity food products and make their innovative mark in the industry for generations to come.

Our customers' stories are as much a part of the Zabar's tradition as are our families' anecdotes. They tell us about how Zabar's provided the brunch for a son's bris, the bagels and lox for a Yom Kippur break-fast, the gefilte fish at their Passover seder, the roast turkey for Thanksgiving, the caviar on New Year's Eve, or the platters for shiva for a loved one. We have even been told of instances where a dying customer specifically requested that the family's shiva be catered by Zabar's. "My mom was adamant," the journalist Alix Wall told us, "that those coming to pay their last respects be well fed."

What continues to make Zabar's special is the feeling that the owners and employees are always looking for new and exciting products for their customers while at the same time maintaining the store's Old New York ambience and passion for customer ser-

vice. This balance between innovation and tradition makes customers of all ages feel like they are part of a larger experience when
they come into the store to make their purchases.

One thing that has significantly changed since my grandparents'
day is that back then the food, the employees, and the customers were predominantly Jewish. Nowadays, the food we sell, our
employees, and our customers come from all over the world. The
culinary universe has become globalized, making it much more
interesting and rewarding for everyone. To paraphrase that famous
1960s ad campaign for Levy's Real Jewish Rye Bread, "You don't
have to be Jewish" to love Zabar's!

I'm proud to be a member of a family that created and nourishes
a New York institution by preserving the personality of the original
store while constantly adapting to new trends, new technologies,
and new health-and-safety regulations. I admire Saul's and Stanley's
dedication to the welfare of their staff, their customers, their family, and their neighborhood in every business decision they make,
and I'm thrilled to see Louis and Lilly's grandchildren and great-
grandchildren carry on the Zabar's traditions. But most of all, I am

(From left to right) *Eli, Saul, Carole, Devon, Judy, me (in hat),*
and Stanley in Key West, 2013. When we gathered to celebrate my mother's
eightieth birthday, the Zabar brothers reminisced with me about their
childhoods and about the store. (ZABAR FAMILY COLLECTION)

Zabar's today, still selling the highest-quality food at the lowest prices,
just as Louis and Lilly did back in 1934. (JUAN C. LOPEZ ESPANTALEON/
)

thankful that Zabar's continues to bring joy and sustenance to so many in a world where most family businesses have disappeared.

A century after my grandparents immigrated to America, their legacy continues in the business they founded, the descendants they nurtured, and the core values they passed down to us all: work hard, support the extended family financially and emotionally, be charitable, and always offer the best quality and the best service at the best price. Beginning in 1934, Zabar's and Manhattan's Upper West Side have lived through difficult times as well as good times together. That's why the store's slogan is NEW YORK IS ZABAR'S · ZABAR'S IS NEW YORK®.

I like to say that Zabar's is the longest-running show on Broadway.

ZABAR'S KEY PLAYERS: THE STAFF

There would be no Zabar's without the loyal and dedicated staff, many of whom have been with the store for decades. They keep the enterprise lively and fresh 365 days a year. With gratitude and affection, I introduce some of them to you.*

Olga Dominguez, Dairy Director

When Olga started working part-time in what was then Zabar's small dairy department, she was seventeen years old and knew nothing about cheese. She had arrived with her family from the Dominican Republic only four years earlier, in 1968. Fifty years later, Olga now presides over one of the largest cheese departments in America. She is particularly excited about the growing number of American artisanal cheeses being produced. When Murray and Stanley gave her carte blanche to expand the cheese department in 1979, it was unusual for a woman to be given such responsibility. Olga fearlessly imported hundreds of French cheeses she had never tasted. She feels privileged when she can help a customer with a purchase for a special occasion, once even creating a wedding cake from a tower of cheese for a thrilled bride. Her manner is so warm and modest that one might never guess she is one of the few Americans to have been inducted into La Guilde Internationale des Fromagers, a prestigious international organization that recognizes and honors cheese experts for their comprehensive knowledge.

Scott Goldshine, General Manager

Scott has seen it all since he started working at Zabar's in 1977, at age seventeen. Over the years, this lifelong New Yorker and chief troubleshooter has managed almost every department, including housewares, grocery, coffee, and front-end. As general manager, he presides over his staff of 230 in seven departments with a calm and cheerful demeanor, and he maintains personal relationships with the store's many suppliers and tradespeople. After more than four decades at Zabar's, Scott continues to find joy in meeting people from all walks of life. Many of his customers turned into friends, including such famous Zabar's stalwarts as Lauren Bacall, Eli Wallach, Anne Jackson, and Ed Bradley. Newer acquaintances include Bruce Willis, Lin-Manuel Miranda, and Pink. What he likes most of all is observing the pleasure Zabar's food brings to them.

Kenneth Hom, Front-End Manager and Coffee Buyer

A New Yorker by birth, Ken fulfills two key roles as a front-end manager and coffee buyer. Every day, he ensures a smooth operation for the cashiers, the stock and floor employees, and the bread and coffee departments staff. Ken got his start in the coffee department in 1984 and still joins Saul in the weekly "cupping" of all the coffees. Nowadays, he's excited about creating a cold brew for the Zabar's Cafe, based on a recipe Saul developed in the 1960s but never produced. He's fascinated by the wide range of people who walk through the doors of Zabar's, from the neighborhood shoppers to superstar actors to politicians and dignitaries. But Ken always maintains a proper New Yorker's casual attitude toward the celebrities. When Jeffrey Loria, the onetime owner of the Florida Marlins, and Marlins pitcher Josh Beckett came to the store, Ken acknowledged them with the briefest eye contact and a quick, pleasant nod.

Tiffany Ludwig, Creative Services

Tiffany has been the artistic director of Zabar's visual presence since 2004, skillfully crafting the graphics that enhance our customers' user experience online and in print. Tiffany was "discovered" when she was teaching a Photoshop class at the Jewish Community Center on the Upper West Side. One of her students was Stanley Zabar, who offered her a consulting job at Zabar's. It took about one second for Tiffany to say yes. Also a fine artist, she is the cocreator, with Renee Piechocki, of a photography and video exhibit entitled *Trappings: Stories of Women, Power and Clothing*.

Patria Morel, Controller and Chief Financial Officer

Pat manages all things financial at Zabar's. She started at the store in 1987 and has worked in a number of capacities over the years. She now oversees human resources, accounts payable and receivable, all contracts, investments, and retirement plans. Always stylish and fit, Pat loves the challenge of putting together all the pieces in the complex puzzle that makes up the Zabar's organization. Her busman's holiday is managing her family finances.

Bernardo Muniz, The Mezzanine Housewares Manager and Buyer

Born in Puerto Rico, Bernardo began his career at Zabar's in 1980, when he was nineteen years old, back when the store occupied a single building. Under Murray Klein's guidance, Bernardo worked his way up from grocery clerk to housewares manager to buyer for The Mezzanine. For people who like to cook, The Mezzanine is like a toy store for adults, so Bernardo is never bored. A good day for Bernardo is when he can help a customer with special housewares needs or requests—the more esoteric, the better.

Tomas Rodriguez, Smoked Fish Manager and Buyer

Tomas was born in the Dominican Republic in 1957, and when he started working at Zabar's thirty years ago, he hardly spoke English. Eventually, he became fluent enough to become an appetizing man behind the fish counter, and he later became Saul's assistant buyer for smoked fish. Under Saul's exacting tutelage, Tomas learned the art of sampling and selecting fish. When Tomas is behind the counter, he stands at the left end, one of the two spots reserved for the most talented lox slicers. It was formerly occupied by the legendary slicer Sam Cohen, and Tomas is a most worthy successor.

Milagros Santiago, Head Cashier Manager

A native New Yorker, Millie has worked at Zabar's since 1981. Unflappable and patient, she rings up customers while at the same time managing the other cashiers and enjoying friendly relationships with her regulars. (Actor and Zabar's customer Laurence Fishburne once took her on a motorcycle ride.) Like so many Zabar's employees, Millie regards coworkers as family—but in her case, one literally is. Millie is married to Bernardo Muniz, The Mezzanine housewares manager and buyer. Like many a romantic couple, Millie and Bernardo met at Zabar's.

David Tait, Senior Manager and Project Manager

This tall, blond Milwaukee native had never been to New York City before he paid his first visit to Zabar's in 1984, in his capacity as a sales representative for the Vie de France croissants that were baked in the middle of the store. He was impressed by what he saw. The service was fast-paced and efficient, with a good dose of New York humor. After meeting with Murray Klein, David tasted his first babka and freshly baked rugelach. Screwing up his courage, he took a number and waited nervously for Sam Cohen to give him his first taste of thinly sliced Nova Scotia salmon. A year and a half later, Murray offered to double whatever David was then being paid if he agreed to come to Zabar's as a manager. Back then, this was David's dream job, and it still is today. As senior manager, David is involved in all daily operations, develops training programs, and maintains systems for personnel. Twenty years ago, wearing his other hat as project manager, David created the gift box and basket program, which he still directs and which has grown into 60 percent of the online shopping business at Zabar's. He is also in charge of physical projects, including the recent renovation of the Zabar's Cafe. After thirty-four years on the job, David still feels that Zabar's food, employees, and customers embody all the energy and excitement that is New York City.

Lawrence Zilko, Information Technology Director

Larry joined Zabar's in 1995 and currently researches, plans, purchases, develops, and implements all of the store's technology, with a particular focus on overseeing the development and design of the Zabar's website. At Stanley's urging, Larry created Zabars.com in 2002; it was one of the industry's first websites for ordering food online. Working at Zabar's makes Larry feel like part of Upper West Side history. He's a member of the Zabar's family on several levels: his grandmother Rose was Louis Zabar's sister and his grandfather Irving Henner was the Zabar's accountant in the 1940s.

ACKNOWLEDGMENTS

The seed for this book began in a memoir-writing class taught by Kaylie Jones at Southampton Writers Conference. In response to an assignment to write from another person's point of view, I conjured the thoughts of my beloved grandmother Lilly Zabar, as she danced the hora at my bat mitzvah reception. This exercise sparked the idea of a history of my family and their business, Zabar's.

At the time, I did not realize what an enormous project it would be to trace and understand more than a century of family life and commerce. Now I know it takes a shtetl of support. This book would not have been possible without the generosity of my relatives in providing memories, archival materials and images, and encouragement. I spent many a Jewish holiday meal quizzing my father, Stanley; my uncle Saul; and my uncle Eli. My mother, Judy, who married into the Zabar family at age nineteen, provided many memories of Lilly, as well as Lilly's recipes. My father's family was incredibly helpful in offering their reminiscences of my grandparents. Phil Leifer, Margaret and Jeff Bary, and my brother, David Zabar, provided invaluable recorded interviews with deceased relatives. Other important sources included the late Sol Henner, Millie Zilko, Anna May Durrell, the late Steve Wagner, Yevgenya and Solomon Zabarko, Sam Zabarko, and Nitza Schwabsky. Joy Watman Segal and the late Andrea Watman proffered essential information about Lilly's family: the Teitelbaums and the Stillmans. Through Jewishgen.org, I found Dr. Dean Echenberg, who led me to a treasure trove of information about the town of Sherbrooke in Canada, where Louis Zabar first arrived in North America. Other non-relatives contributed their memories, including Jewel Stern, Sam Siporin, Aihud Pevsner, and Steve Zion. Hillary Matlin, Horace Mann

School Archivist, provided invaluable material. I am grateful to Roger Klein and Deb Himmelfarb for information about their father, Murray Klein, and cousin Aaron Klein. The basis for information on Ostropolia was two books by relatives on our extended family tree: *Our Family History* by Ida F. Kaiser (self-published in 1982) and *The Jewish Families of Ostropol* by Deborah Glassman (an e-book published in 2015). A communication from Mattis Kovalenko, of Montreal, arrived like manna from heaven. While researching his ancestors in Ostropolia, he came upon Mordko Leib Zabarka's untitled account, in Yiddish, of the pogroms in Ostropolia on the website of the Jewish Distribution Committee (JDC). He ingeniously identified the author as a relative of the owners of Zabar's and emailed the invaluable statement to Saul. Thank you to the professional translators I engaged and to Dan Dubno, who located the JDC's English translation. I am also indebted to the numerous librarians and archivists who provided guidance and materials during my research.

This book would not exist without the "Jewish geography" connections among David Abramson, Marc Russ Federman, Gail Hochman, and Emily Forland, which led me to my amazing agent, Jody Kahn, at Brandt & Hochman. Jody had such faith in the book that she buoyed me when I was ready to give in to discouragement. She helped me craft the proposal and sold the book, guiding me astutely throughout the process with unflagging optimism.

I wandered in the prosaic desert until Michelle Wildgen became my editor extraordinaire. She elegantly enhanced my prose while preserving my voice. Altie Karper, editorial director of Schocken Books, believed in this book and had the patience to wait until it bloomed into fruition. She used her incredible expertise to polish my efforts. Her sage advice as we proceeded to publication was invaluable. My thanks also to the rest of the Schocken team: jacket designer Kelly Blair, associate managing editor Cat Courtade, marketer Sara Eagle, copyeditor Deborah Weiss Geline, text designer Betty Lew, publisher Lisa Lucas, publicist Sarah New, production manager Peggy Samedi, and production editor Melissa Yoon. Julia Moskin, a born-and-bred Upper West Sider and food journalist, was the perfect choice to write the excellent foreword. Many thanks to the Authors Guild for reviewing my contracts and to my friend and neighbor Judy Bass, media and entertainment attorney, for her wise guidance.

For my grandmother, food was love. This book would not be complete without Lilly's recipes. She cooked from memory, and I thank my mother for writing the recipes down while Lilly was alive. Luck was with me when I met Monita Buchwald, a Metropolitan Museum of Art colleague, fellow Barnard alum, and former professional recipe tester, who became a dear friend and volunteered to test and edit Lilly's recipes. My gratitude to her is endless, and I am also thankful to the relatives and friends who executed some of the dishes, including my husband, Mark Mariscal; my sister, Sandy Zabar; my daughter, Marguerite Mariscal; and my friends Linda Kartoz-Doochin, Chris Benter, Beth and Dustin Wees, Lisa Hess and Ted Pettus, Carol Loewenson and Catherine Kurland. Many thanks to Eli Zabar and Devon Fredericks, and Tiffany Ludwig for providing additional recipes.

I am indebted to family, friends, and colleagues at The Metropolitan Museum of Art, who never tired of asking how the book was going and assuring me that it would get done. I appreciate all who read drafts along the way, including Saul and Carole Zabar, Stanley and Judith Zabar, Eli Zabar and Devon Fredericks, Mark Mariscal, Cynthia Schaffner, Hannah Shearer, Monita Buchwald, Barbara Greene, Ted Pettus, Yona Zeldis McDonough, Barbara Glauber, and especially Catherine Kurland. I value the comments and encouragement from my fellow aspiring writers in Kaylie Jones's and Charles Salzberg's classes, especially those who told me to "zhuzh it up."

Long before the project was finished, Stacey Spector and Ira Brind had such confidence in me, they hosted my first book talk.

I so appreciate the unceasing assistance from the staff at Zabar's in this endeavor. Managers Scott Goldshine and David Tait answered my constant questions with patience and enthusiasm. I am eternally grateful to art director Tiffany Ludwig for cheerfully providing numerous archival and contemporary images for the book. I value Juan C. Lopez Espantaleon's mouthwatering photographs of Zabar's delicacies. My talented nephew Willie Zabar, the store's social media manager, went above and beyond in photographing the longtime key employees and creating a podcast interview with me. Of course, Zabar's would not be Zabar's without its loyal customers. I am so grateful to those who answered my requests for anecdotes.

I could not have arrived in the promised land of book completion without the emotional and physical support of my husband, Mark Mariscal, my rock of ages, who makes each day a culinary delight with his superb cooking skills. Our children, Henry and Marguerite, sustained me emotionally and kept me current with the contemporary foodie scene. My siblings, David and Sandy, and their families cheered me on. And most of all, my enthusiastic and loving parents, Judy and Stanley Zabar, continue to set an example for all of us on how to live a life of generosity, friendship, curiosity, and celebration.

INDEX

Page numbers in *italics* refer to illustrations.

A NOTE ABOUT THE TYPE

This text of this book has been set in Amerigo, a typeface designed in 1986 by award-winning Dutch graphic and type designer, author, and teacher Gerard Unger (1942–2018). Along with his many font designs, Unger also designed special digits for the Dutch telephone directories in 1984 and his experience working on coins and stamps is evident in Amerigo's flared, tapered stroke endings that give the typeface the feel of being engraved on a hard surface.

Composed by North Market Street Graphics, Lancaster, Pennsylvania

Printed and bound by LSC Harrisonburg, Harrisonburg, Virginia

Designed by Betty Lew

The

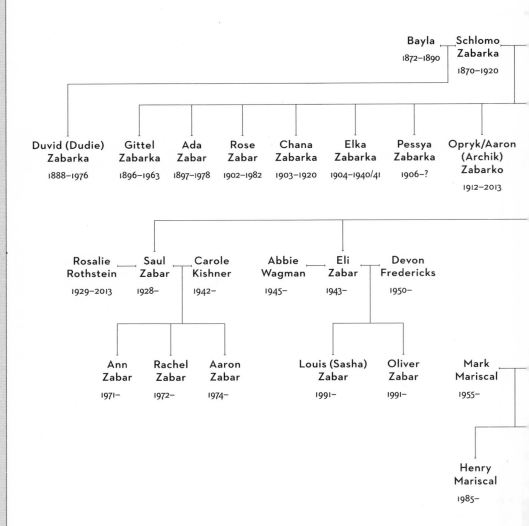

Bayla
1872–1890

Schlomo Zabarka
1870–1920

Duvid (Dudie) Zabarka
1888–1976

Gittel Zabarka
1896–1963

Ada Zabar
1897–1978

Rose Zabar
1902–1982

Chana Zabarka
1903–1920

Elka Zabarka
1904–1940/41

Pessya Zabarka
1906–?

Opryk/Aaron (Archik) Zabarko
1912–2013

Rosalie Rothstein
1929–2013

Saul Zabar
1928–

Carole Kishner
1942–

Abbie Wagman
1945–

Eli Zabar
1943–

Devon Fredericks
1950–

Ann Zabar
1971–

Rachel Zabar
1972–

Aaron Zabar
1974–

Louis (Sasha) Zabar
1991–

Oliver Zabar
1991–

Mark Mariscal
1955–

Henry Mariscal
1985–